You're Nothing but a Number

Why achieving great credit scores should be on your list of wealth building strategies

By
John R. Ulzheimer

❧ Foreword ❧

In ancient times, lending was based upon familiarity: people extended credit to people they knew, or at least people known to them or their drinking or hunting buddies. While in many cases the amount due was somewhat reasonable (a number of merciful potentates actually limited interest to no more than 20 percent), if a borrower was in a pinch he could always settle a debt by selling his wife or children into slavery. Some spouses and offspring even had the good fortune to live in kingdoms where enlightened rulers limited the number of years one had to endure indentured servitude to no more than three.

As "B.C." became "A.D." cultures all around the world continued to facilitate lending and borrowing. In 18th century Britain, traveling drapers known as "tallymen" would go door-to-door selling clothes to housewives on credit. They'd collect some money "now" and some money when they returned. Two points should be made about this method of credit: first, it was a personal relationship; second, completely settling a debt back then was actually considered a form of severing a relationship. Maintaining some debt kept creditors' relationships with debtors ongoing and personal (though it did help them lose favor with husbands who didn't care for the debt that was being accrued when they were away at work).

Fast forward to 2007 - skip all that relational stuff and save the Tallyman for the next Harry Belafonte record. To paraphrase Sinatra, **"You're nothing but a number, kid."**

Today, the American system of credit reduces your entire life to a series of numbers—and ultimately a score based on your debt, payment history, the number of credit cards in your name, the amount of credit you could be using that you actually are using and more. All of these things are tabulated and cross-tabulated for the sake of determining your credit score. If you have a good score, you'll be able to secure loans and insurance without a hassle, get better interest rates that make your life easier and more affordable, even have a pathway to a better job. A bad credit score can ruin your life. You might not be forced to sell off your first-born child, but you will find yourself dealing with higher interest rates and worse yet, unable to find anyone willing to loan you money.

Mastering today's credit system is sort of like a numbers game in Vegas. The more you know coming to the table, the less likely you'll be caught off guard and ultimately, lose the house to the dealer.

Here's one they don't teach you in school (I never really understood why) - *the right credit portfolio can mean as much to your life as the right investment portfolio*. So, how do you build the "right" portfolio? Here is where life imitates art. The most famous line from the movie *Field of Dreams* was, "If you build it, they will come." In the world of credit, the inescapable truth is: if you don't build it, they will run.

You need to begin at the beginning. Learn as much as possible about the system: what affects your credit score, how to stop the bleeding, and how to quickly and intelligently rebuild and/or enhance your score. Separate the facts from the myths. Simply put, discover how the folks who give you credit keep score.

If I had a dime for every credit book written by every "credit expert," I guess I wouldn't need credit. Some are pretty good. Some are pretty lame. And, some are….well…..let's just say they look impressive on the shelf.

This book is different because its author is different than the other guys. In the movie *Wall Street,* Gordon Gekko (Michael Douglas) ordered Bud Fox (Charlie Sheen) to "stop giving me information and start getting me information." *You're Nothing but a Number* wasn't written by a guy who knows a guy who knows the story. It was written by the guy who has helped write the story.

John Ulzheimer spent six years at Equifax, seven years at Fair Isaac and a significant number of years educating consumers to help themselves. An inside guy who has built the actual FICO scoring models, developed and implemented consumer credit education programs and contributed to several books, he has seen the best and worst of what can happen to those who understand how to build and maintain strong and healthy credit histories as well as folks who either don't know or can't handle the score. He has written hundreds of articles, given thousands of interviews, participated in countless roundtables and taught at several universities. He has traveled the country not with a tally stick but rather a storehouse of invaluable knowledge that has de-mystified the process and helped hundreds of thousands of consumers better understand where they are, how to protect what they have or rebuild what they – or circumstances beyond their control – have damaged.

He knows the score. And, if you read this gem of a book, you will too.

> Adam Levin
> Former Director of the New Jersey Division of
> Consumer Affairs
> President/CEO, Credit.com, Inc.

⚘ Introduction ⚘

When I was a young man, my parents told me that someday I'd have to borrow money from someone other than them. Clearly, they said this because they recognized that most of us don't have the amount of cash it takes to buy large ticket items. In order for me to be able to borrow money to buy a car, a house, or anything else, I'd have to be sure our local banker was so impressed with my qualifications that he would have no choice but to approve my loan application. This meant that I needed to show, among other things, a record of paying my bills and creditors on time.

Like most young people, I thought I knew everything. I was sorely mistaken. What in the world was this "credit report" they needed to see? And who were these companies whose sole function was to compile, maintain, and sell my highly sensitive personal information? And what in the world was this "728" the banker kept referring to?

Nobody ever taught me about this stuff in school. I successfully completed sixteen years of it, and not one class ever addressed credit reports or credit scores. I learned about algebra, U.S history, the art of debate, and how to properly craft a sentence, but nobody taught me how to build, manage, and protect my personal credit and credit scores – skills that I'd rely upon for roughly 80% of my life. I learned how to do these things like everyone else did…through trial and error….and more error and more error.

Fast forward to today. I've now worked in the consumer credit world for over sixteen years, with six of those years spent working for one of the credit reporting agencies and another seven working for *the* credit scoring company. I've built credit scores. I've taught lenders how to make the best use of credit information, and I've even taught consumers what makes credit scores tick. I've seen tens of thousands of credit reports, and I've heard even more sob stories from individuals about why they're credit report is so full of negative information.

And in my time and travels I've come to several undisputable conclusions...

- Other than your employer, the credit reporting agencies have more influence over your life than any other company. They are simply the most powerful companies in the United States.

- We are grossly undereducated when it comes to anything related to credit. Seriously. We know very little. And those who think they know are the worst because they're spreading what they think they know...which is mostly incorrect.

The problem with credit education is that very few people are actually qualified to teach this information. To do so requires an intimate knowledge of the credit industry. But most insiders aren't interested in sharing what they know because educating people isn't normally a profitable business venture. In fact, keeping us uneducated is much more profitable because we're likely to pay higher interest rates and higher insurance premiums. And since we're undereducated, we have an insatiable appetite for access to our own credit information, which can be very expensive for us and very profitable for the credit reporting agencies. We have to see what someone else is saying about us...and we're willing to pay for it.

I had an hour to speak at a private high school's senior assembly in Atlanta in 2006. I ended up talking to 100 boys and then 100 girls. The first question I asked them was, "How many of you know what a credit reporting agency is?" None of them raised their hands. My next question was, "Next year, when you're in college, how many of you will get your own credit cards?" All of them raised their hands. See what I mean? That's grossly -- or, better put, dangerously -- undereducated. It's the credit equivalent of sticking a bunch of people who don't know how to drive on a freeway during rush hour. They will get overwhelmed, and the pain of learning the hard way will be severe.

•• What's on your credit reports isn't as important as the interpretation of what's on your credit reports. Read that sentence again, please. It's important. Nobody cares that you have late payments and nobody cares that you have debt. What they do care about is how that information is interpreted through either a credit scoring model or some other type of model. If you are deemed to be "risky"based on an interpretation of your credit reports, then lenders will decline your credit applications or counter with less attractive offers. And there's very little you can do about it.

•• Your income is irrelevant, your debt to income is irrelevant, your net worth is irrelevant, and your assets and holdings are irrelevant. None of these things matter one lick when it comes to your credit reports or your credit scores. You might have great "capacity," but it won't matter. Capacity, in the lending world, is your ability to make a payment. So, if you have a car payment of $1,000 each month, you're expected to prove that you make enough money to have $1,000 to make the payment. Capacity isn't the same as creditworthiness.

This fact leads to some really funny stories about wealthy people being declined for loans while their maids and butlers are getting 0% interest offers left and right.

◆ Your story isn't important. Lenders and insurance companies simply don't care that you got laid off or you got divorced or your dog ate your bills. To them, it's all about whether or not they'll make or lose money by doing business with you. If, in their evaluation, they think they will lose money on your account, then you're not getting approved-- period! If they can figure out some way to price out your account so they'll make money (with interest rates, down payments, or some other security), you'll get approved. It's very cut and dry.

◆ When pushed to share information, the credit industry's first reaction is usually one of resistance. It has taken legislation to give us access to our own credit reports, and in some cases we're still buying access...TO OUR OWN INFOR-MATION.

If you think about the credit reporting agencies and what they do, it's a very comical business model no other companies use. They are given your information from lenders for free. That's right, they don't pay lenders for your payment and account information. Then they take that information and sell it back to other lenders for a fee. And, they also sell it to you for a fee whenever they have the opportunity to do so.

Think about that for a moment. Let's say I went around your neighborhood and got everyone's phone numbers. Then I compiled all of those phone numbers in a book and sold the books to everyone in the neighborhood for $12.95 each. That's basically what the credit reporting agencies do. How great is that?

◆ Every credit report is inaccurate. I realize this is a bold statement. Some of you may have just rolled your eyes, but I stand by my comment. I'll dedicate an entire chapter to support my argument. I believe you will agree with me once you're done reading. Let's just say this one will really burn you up.

My goal in writing this book is to expose you to information that simply isn't available unless you work in key positions at one of a very small handful of companies with access to policies and procedures that aren't made public. Let me be very clear about something. What I'm going to share with you will probably tick you off, and it should. And as I always say before I present this material in my classes or seminars, where I'm always the least popular person in the room: Please don't shoot the messenger! This unvarnished exposé on the credit industry is just what you've been missing, and exactly what you need. So, from inside the walls...enjoy.

Table of Contents

Table of Contents

Chapter 1

Consumer Reporting Agencies

Y ou'll notice that I titled this chapter "Consumer Reporting Agencies" rather than "Credit Reporting Agencies." Legally speaking, any company that collects and then shares information about your credit, insurance worthiness, or reputation with another company or person is considered to be a consumer reporting agency. While many of us are at least somewhat familiar with the three major credit reporting agencies – Equifax, Transunion and Experian – few have ever heard of the two other consumer reporting agencies I'll profile this book. If you take the time to learn about how they operate, you'll be a step ahead of tens of millions of people.

Let's get started…

As I noted in the Introduction, Consumer Reporting Agencies (and more specifically Credit Reporting Agencies) act as data warehouses. They gather information from many sources, standardize it, then market and sell it to people and companies that are allowed to buy it. In the credit world, there are three primary companies that do this: Equifax, TransUnion and Experian. Though we'll talk more about them later, it's important to start becoming familiar with their names. Any book about credit that's worth its price has to mention these companies in the first chapter.

Here's how it works

Credit reporting agencies (also referred to as "credit bureaus") are only interested in certain information about you. It has to be data that they can legally collect and sell and it also has to be data their customers are interested in buying. For example, John's Bank isn't really interested in the fact that you like to water ski. But, they are interested in the fact that you owe Dave's Bank $15,000 for a ski boat.

So how do the credit bureaus get your information? It's actually fairly simple. Lenders send it to them. They normally send them your information every month with the current month's information overlaying the last month's information. You might also be surprised to learn that lenders don't charge the credit bureaus a dime for your information. They gladly give it to them free of charge.

Once the credit bureaus receive your information, they magically tie it to your "file." Whenever another company wants to buy your credit report, the credit bureaus know to include the Dave's Bank account information.

Why would lenders give their information (or your information) away for free? They consider it leverage over you. If you have a credit card with John's Bank and you don't feel like making your payment one month, John's Bank is going to say "Fine, then we're going to report that information to the credit bureaus for everyone else to see." All of a sudden making your payments on time takes on an added importance, doesn't it? If your payments are late, then everyone else will know about it.

What makes up my credit report?

Your credit report is made up of several things, including your personal identifying information, loan and credit card account information, and public record and collection information. The dates and companies with which you applied for credit are also on your credit reports. These are called "inquiries."

Loan and Credit Card Account Information

The bulk of the information in your credit reports is credit and loan information. When you take out a loan or sign up for a credit card, the account and payment information will eventually appear in your credit reports. This is what an account will typically look like once it lands in your credit reports.

John's Bank

Account #:	193xx-0939-xx	Date Reported:	02/07
Type:	Revolving	Current Balance:	$5,000
Pay Status:	Current	Credit Limit:	$10,000
Date Opened:	05/04	Previous Late Payments:	Pays As Agreed

As you can see, it's a very complete description of the type and history of your account. Everything that you see here is fair game, meaning anyone who can legally purchase one of your credit reports will see all of this information. And, despite the fact that this is your information, there's nothing you can do to prevent it from showing up. You have no choice in the matter.

Public Record Information

Public record information is different from loan and account information. First, there are no lenders to report this information, and courthouses aren't staffed to send your credit-related public records to the credit bureaus. Second, not all public records make it to your credit reports. In fact, the majority of your public records never grace the pages of your credit reports.

Only public records that are of interest to lenders make it to your credit reports. And what records do you think would be of interest to a lender? Bankruptcy, judgments and liens. For example, if you file for bankruptcy, or a lender sues you and wins, or the IRS files a tax lien against you, this information will become public record. You can go down to your local courthouse and look up this information at your leisure. It's public!

Public Record Information

Lien Filed 07/04: Hall County	Satisfied Judgement Filed 01/02;
ID Number-43211	Hall County
Amount-$18754	ID Number-352719
Class-State	Defendant-John Consumer
Released 10/04; Verified 07/04	Amount-$9567
	Plaintiff-ABC Real Estate
Bankruptcy Filed 05/04	Satisfied 02/02; Verified 03/02
Southern District Ct	
ID Number-849BR54	
Liabilities-$19463;	
Discharged; Assets-$830	

And how does all of this get in your credit reports since there are no lenders to report it? There are companies called "Public Record Vendors" that gather relevant public record information and send it to the credit bureaus. The credit bureaus pay them a fee to gather this information for them. This is the only information on your credit reports that the credit bureaus pay for.

A word to the wise...there are never any good public records that are reported to the credit reporting agencies. They are all bad.

Collections

If you have accounts with a lender and you chose to stop paying them, one of the options the lender has is to sell the account (or consign it) to another company called a Collection Agency. Collection agencies specialize in collecting money from people who don't pay. One of the ways they can convince people to pay up is to threaten reporting the collection account to the credit reporting agencies.

As with public record information, there are never any good collection accounts reported to the collection agencies.

Collection Information

John's Collection Agency	Account #: 123456789
(555) 555-5555	Original Balance: $500
Original Creditor:	Current Balance: $578
John's Auto Mall	Date Filed: 05/2005

Companies that Pulled Your Credit Reports and When

Become very familiar with the word "Inquiry." Inquiry is a very common term in the lending world. It's the listing on your credit file of who pulled your credit report and on what date. That's all it is. An inquiry looks like this:

Companies That Requested Your Credit File

Chase	01-17-08	Discover	06-08-08
JuniperBk	08-15-08	Cingular	04-06-08
CapitalOne	07-24-08	John'sMtg	03-11-08

This information constitutes the bulk of what makes up our credit reports. A complete credit report example can be seen on the following page.

SAMPLE CREDIT REPORT

Personal Identification Information

Etheridge Plum
123 Small Town Blvd.
Anytown, GA 30326

Social Security Number: 123-45-6789
Date of Birth: January 31, 1968

Previous Address(es):
745 Main Sreet, Anytown, GA 30319
P.O. Box xxxx, Orlando, FL 32801
Last Reported Employer: CSR, John's Bank

Public Record Information

Lien Filed 07/04: Hall County
ID Number-43211
Amount-$18754
Class-State
Released 10/04; Verified 07/04

Bankruptcy Filed 05/18/04
Southern District Ct
ID Number-849BR54
Liabilities-$19463;
Discharged; Assets-$830

Satisfied Judgement Filed 01/02; Hall
County
ID Number-352719
Defendant-Etheridge Plum
Amount-$9567
Plaintiff-ABC Real Estate
Satisfied 02/02; Verified 03/02

Collection Account Information

John's Collection Agency
(555) 555-5555
Original Creditor:
John's Auto Mall

Account #: 123456789
Original Balance: $500
Current Balance: $578
Date Filed: 05/2005

Credit Account Information

Company Name	Account #	Type	Date Opened	Date of Last Activity	Credit Limit/High Credit	Current Balance	Pay Status	Date Reported	Previous Payment History
John's Bk	193xx-xx	I	05/04	02/07	$26,423	$6,538	Current	02/07	30 days past due 1 year ago
Discover	234xx-xx	R	03/98	01/07	$10,000	$1,268	Current	01/07	Pays As Agreed
ABC Mtg	567xx-xx	I	04/96	12/06	$230,000		Current	12/06	60 days past due 1 year ago

Companies That Requested Your Credit File

Chase	01-17-08	Discover	06-08-08
JuniperBk	08-15-08	Cingular	04-06-08
CapitalOne	07-24-08	John'sMtg	03-11-08

The Players

As I mentioned earlier, there are a very limited number of companies that compile, store, and then sell your credit-related information. They are:

Equifax

Equifax is based in Atlanta, GA, and has been around in one form or another for over 100 years. It is a public company whose stock symbol is EFX.

Experian

Experian is based in Costa Mesa, CA, and has been around since it completed the acquisition of the credit data once owned by TRW's old credit services division. It is a UK company and as of early 2007 is not traded publicly in the United States.

TransUnion

TransUnion, or "TU" as it's commonly called, is based in Chicago, IL. It's owned by perhaps the second wealthiest family in Chicago, behind Oprah Winfrey's. Since it is family-owned, it is not publicly traded (as of late 2007).

Rather than launching into separate descriptions, I'll save a few trees and time by saying this: they all do the same thing. They'll argue that they offer different things to different companies, but the reality is they all have the same core business, which is to compile and sell credit information, products, and services that are derivatives of credit information.

They all have credit files on roughly 250,000,000 people in the U.S. and do business in multiple other countries. For example, TransUnion and Equifax also have Canadian credit reporting agencies.

The Other Two

A fourth credit-reporting agency is Innovis Data Solutions, which is owned by the Credit Bureau of Columbus, located in Columbus, OH. It is also called CBCInnovis. It jumped into the fray and decided to compete with the big three credit bureaus and has made some inroads. Today, it's still considered "the fourth credit bureau," which isn't a great advertisement, but that's not what this book is about. The fact that it may have YOUR personal information in its database is what's important.

The last of our important companies is ChoicePoint. It is not a credit reporting agency. It is, however, by legal definition, a consumer reporting agency. Years ago, Equifax had an Insurance Services division. That division spun off into its own company, which was named ChoicePoint, based in Atlanta, GA.

ChoicePoint is to insurance companies what Equifax is to lenders. Insurance companies want to know certain things about you before they will give you auto or homeowner's insurance policies. Specifically, they want to know what kind of insurance claim history you have, just like a lender wants to know what kind of loan history you have. That's exactly what ChoicePoint sells: your insurance claim history.

Just as lenders send your loan history to the credit bureaus, insurance companies send your claim history to ChoicePoint. The information is compiled and then sold off to any other company that has a legal right to access the information. There will be more about ChoicePoint later.

What should you do today?

It's very important that you periodically get a copy of exactly what these companies are saying about you. It's in your best interest to do this multiple times each year to make sure that your information is accurate. You can do this by getting a copy of your credit reports, which are free at least once a year thanks to a new federal law signed in 2003 and implemented throughout 2005, the FACT ACT. We'll talk more about your rights and what to do if you find errors in Chapter 7.

To get your Equifax, Experian, and TransUnion credit reports for free, go to www.annualcreditreport.com. Or, if you don't have Internet access, you can call 1-877-322-8228.

Innovis doesn't make it as easy as the big three. You have to request your report by mail. The address is:

Innovis Consumer Assistance
P.O. Box 1358
Columbus, OH 43216-1358

You can get a copy of your ChoicePoint file in their system via the Internet. The website address is www.choicetrust.com.

Chapter 2

Credit Scoring 101:
The Basics...and the Advanced

The Basics

On the surface, credit scoring is fairly simple. Your credit information is run through a credit-scoring model, which spits out a number. This number is essentially your credit report's grade. That grade is delivered along with your credit reports and is used by lenders and insurance companies to assess your level of risk. Very simple, right?

> *"Lenders don't make a dime unless you pay them back, eventually. That's their risk when doing business with you."*

Your credit score is a three-digit number that ranges from somewhere around 300 on the low end to 850 on the high end. You want this score to be as high as possible. The higher your score, the less of a risk you look like to a lender or insurance company. And, a lesser risk translates into a better deal for you. A lower score means that the bank or insurance company will be taking a bigger chance if they approve your application. And, as compensation for assuming that bigger risk, banks will charge you more in interest and insurance companies will charge you higher premiums. In fact, you may be living in a neighborhood where all of the houses cost about the same...but I guarantee you that everyone who lives there isn't making the same home payment each month. It's also very unlikely that everyone who lives there is being charged the same amount to insure their homes.

So how do I get a good credit score?

This is the million-dollar question. Well, you don't get a good credit score; you *earn* a good (or great) credit score. Contrary to popular opinion, a good credit score isn't your right. It's something that you must earn just like a grade awarded in school. Just showing up to class only gets you so far. You have to work at getting good grades. The same is true for credit scoring. You've got to work to earn and maintain a good score.

Unlike grades, however, credit scores remain a constant factor in a person's life. As long as you require the services of lenders and insurance companies, they'll rely on credit scores in order to determine what they are willing to offer to you. That means if you start applying for credit in your late teens or early 20s and stop applying for credit when you turn 60 or 70, your credit and credit scores will be fair game for all of those companies to see for nearly half a century. All of a sudden that grade seems pretty important now, doesn't it?

Remember, your credit scores are a summary of the credit information found on your credit report. If your credit information doesn't paint a flattering picture of you, your credit scores won't either. So, how do you establish solid credit information that will score well? We'll address that topic in Chapter 6.

The Advanced

There are folks who, like me, have a more inquisitive appetite with respect to credit scores. The rest of this chapter is for them. This is the stuff that gets me called "geek" or "egghead," which is fine. This is the real magic behind credit scores. If you don't have at least a basic understanding of what makes credit scores tick, it's going to be more difficult for you to earn impressive scores.

Contrary to popular thinking, credit scores are not new. They've actually been around for decades. Credit scoring is simply a process whereby data or other consumer variables are quantified through research and then implemented into some sort of underwriting process or system. So, in English, that simply means an applicant's information is turned into numbers. Then those numbers are added together and the sum is your credit score. Lenders and insurance companies set their approval and pricing policies around those scores.

So what goes into building a credit score?

Don't fall asleep on me now. This is important stuff – if you ever want to truly understand why your scores are as good or bad as they are, you'll need to know this. Once you understand how the scoring models are built, you'll have a new appreciation for how you should manage your credit.

The process is called regression. Don't bother looking it up, because the definition won't make a lot of sense in relation to credit scoring. So, for the purposes of clarity, we'll make up a phrase just for this chapter: credit score regression analysis.

Any company or person that builds credit-scoring models could be referred to as a mind reader. They are essentially trying to build a crystal ball that lenders can look into and see the future payment patterns of their applicants. Their challenge is to make the best crystal ball possible. And, the most powerful tool that can be used to tell what someone is going to do in the future is… what? What they've done in the past of course. That's regression, credit score style.

The most powerful crystal balls take into account what you've done in the past. Let's look at an analogy. If I came up to you and wanted to bet you $100 that I could throw a football 50 yards, what would be your first question before deciding whether or not to take my bet? It should be, "Have you ever thrown a ball 50 yards before?" If my answer is yes, then you might not want to bet. If I've never even gotten close to 50 yards, you probably want to throw your money down because chances are I won't do it this time, either. It's a much safer bet if you have a little information, isn't it? This is why credit scoring models are built the way that they are. How you've managed your credit in the past is the #1 indicator of how you're going to manage your credit in the future.

Throughout the process of credit score regression analysis, the model developers will look for things that the "good" credit risks have in common. They'll also look for things that "bad" credit risks have in common. What they end up with is a meaty list of predictive credit related questions (also known as "characteristics").

"Predictive" is really the key term. Anyone can throw together a short consumer questionnaire, sell it to a lender, and expect it to distinguish between a good and bad credit risk. But if the questions they're asking to applicants aren't predictive of future credit behavior, the questionnaire and its results are worthless.

That said, a credit-scoring model is really just a series of questions that your credit reports have to answer. For every answer given, points are assigned and your score is calculated. In order for any question/characteristic to make it into a quality credit-scoring model, the data has to be highly predictive of future credit risk.

Can you pick out a few of the predictive questions that are a part of any good credit-scoring model?

1. What color is your car?
2. Do you miss payments on loans?
3. How much credit card debt do you have?
4. Do you like fishing?
5. Would you rather have a dog or a cat?
6. How many loans have you applied for in the past 12 months?

It doesn't take a statistician to figure out which questions are going to be valuable when determining credit risk, but if you need an answer key, here it is: #2, #3 and #6 are components of any good credit scoring model. The other questions are not.

A good credit-scoring model will have a library of hundreds, maybe thousands, of those predictive questions to choose from. They don't all make it into the model, however. Instead, only the most predictive questions or the most predictive combinations of questions are utilized.

So how do I earn points?

Now that you have a basic understanding of how a predictive question is used in a model, it's time to learn about another new phrase: the variable. This refers to any answer given to a predictive question used in a credit scoring model. These answers can "vary," hence the term "variable."

Let's take one of the predictive questions from our earlier list and come up with some possible variables. We'll use question #3, "How much credit card debt do you have?"

Here is a common way the variables are set up for that type of question:

How much credit card debt do you have?

> < $10,000
> $10,001 - $25,000
> $25,001 - $50,000
> $50,001 - $100,000
> > $100,000

What you have here are five possible answers or variables to the question about credit card debt. And each of those variables is worth a different number of points. Here's an example of how those points could be assigned.

> < $10,000 = 100 points
> $10,001 - $25,000 = 75 points
> $25,001 - $50,000 = 50 points
> $50,001 - $100,000 = 25 points
> > $100,000 = 0 points

Not to get ahead of ourselves, but you may have noticed that the number of points you earned goes down as your credit card debt increases. What that should tell you is that having a lot of credit card debt means you are a higher credit risk than someone who doesn't. This not only makes statistical sense but also common sense.

In addition to the credit card example above, there are many other predictive questions and variables that look similar to what you have here. And in order for anyone to earn and maintain solid credit scores, he or she has to do well across the board and earn as many points as possible. That's where great scores come from.

Chapter 3

Who Cares?

So what caused you to buy this book? You had a reason, yes? What was it? Why do you care about credit reporting and credit scoring? This is dry stuff, folks. It's not like you're reading a Tom Clancy or a Stephen King. This is a book about credit.

Here's the deal. If you are reading this book, it's likely that you fall into one of the following categories. You have bad credit and you're looking for a way to improve or rebuild it. You don't have any credit and you're looking for a way to establish credit for the first time. Or maybe you're like my father...the ultimate planner...and you are going to make a major purchase and want to get the best interest rate possible. Or, you're like me and you find this stuff fascinating, and since you're going to be scored for about 80% of your life, you believe it necessary to understand the rules.

Whatever your reason, it doesn't really matter. What matters is that you should care and you should care a lot. You simply cannot avoid the influence of credit reporting and credit scoring. No matter how hard you try, you're in the system and will be in the system until you die. Remember what I said in the introduction. The most powerful companies in America are the ones that preside over your life by maintaining your credit.

Don't believe me? Here are a few examples of what your credit reports and credit scores influence. Any of these sound important to you?

- Getting a home loan or any sort of home equity loan

- Getting a car loan or lease

- Getting a student loan

- Getting homeowner's or auto insurance

- Getting any sort of credit card, whether it be a bank card, retail store card, or a gas card

- Getting cellular service

- Leasing an apartment

- Whether or not you'll be required to make a deposit when you sign up for public utilities (power, gas, water)

- Getting a savings or checking account and a debit card

- Getting and keeping a job

- Your insurance premium on your auto or homeowner's policies

- Your interest rates on any of the above listed loans.

And if you think you can find a lender, employer, or insurance company that doesn't use credit reports or credit scores, good luck. You'd have better luck finding the Holy Grail. All lenders and insurance companies in this country use some sort of grading system to determine whether they will grant you any sort of credit or insurance. And all employers have the legal right to pull your credit reports as part of their employment screening process.

The cost of credit reports has been decreasing for many years. As such, companies that couldn't afford to use them now can and are. Did you know that some places won't let you have a library card without first seeing your credit report? The use of credit reports and scores has spread so much that it's simply impossible to escape their influence.

So, the answer to the question "Who cares?" is "Everyone cares." Everyone who has some sort of influence over your financial life has access to your credit reports and credit scores. In order to get the best possible interest rates, terms, or insurance premiums, you had better manage your credit so that it paints a glowing picture of you as a potential debtor or insurance holder.

Does it really matter that much?

If you're like me, you need to see the numbers before you start to really understand.

If you wanted to borrow $250,000 to buy a house, financed over 30 years (which is typical), and you had a credit score of 670 (which most people consider good, but which is actually below average), your payment each month would be somewhere around $1,884. Your interest rate would be about 7.2%*.

If your credit score was 720 (which is only an average score), your interest rate would drop to around 6.5%*, leaving you with a $1,575 monthly payment. That's a difference in credit scores of only 50 points, but it equates to a difference in house payment each month of $309. That means every year you would spend an extra $3,708 simply because your credit score wasn't up to snuff. That's $37,080 more over 10 years, and \$111,240 if you paid the loan over the full 30 years.

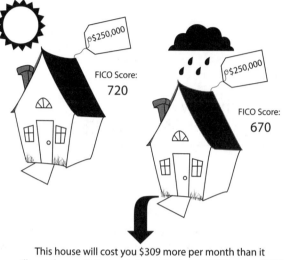

This house will cost you \$309 more per month than it will cost the guy living next door who has a FICO® score of 720.
*These figures are typical with the rates commonly available in early 2007.

It's the same exact house!! But for the person with the lower credit score it will cost much more. That's why you should care.

Chapter 4

Divorce and Why It Will Almost Always Trash Your Credit Scores

I think most people understand and accept that certain things will have a negative impact on their credit scores. Missing payments, excessive debt, and filing for bankruptcy are all common sense reasons for why credit and credit scores suffer. You don't need me to tell you that; you've probably figured it out already.

However, one of the reasons that people get so frustrated and angry about credit scoring is the system will sometimes throw them a curveball. Something that they didn't expect and wasn't obvious. Divorce is one of the curveballs.

In many (if not most) cases, a divorce will ruin your credit reports and credit scores for many years, making it difficult to borrow money at decent interest rates. What makes this a travesty is that it doesn't have to happen. Still, by the time divorcing spouses find out what they've done to their own credit, it's far too late to do anything about it. They both have to go through the process of rebuilding their credit.

Here's the problem: when you're going through the process of a divorce, you are operating under the authority of the divorce court.

Most people make the assumption that whatever the court decides is final and binding on all parties, including all of the couple's lenders. Unfortunately, this is not the case.

As hard as it is to believe, simply because the judge says (or decrees) that one of the divorcing spouses is to be responsible for a joint loan, a credit card, or some other account's payment, does not mean that the other spouse is off the hook. In that situation, the most a person can do is hope that the responsible party will pay. If not, as often happens, BOTH spouse's credit suffers.

Lenders will not honor the court's assignment of payment responsibility. If you and your ex-spouse signed contracts when opening up joint accounts, both parties are still financially liable for the debt regardless of what the judge says. This isn't something that most divorce attorneys typically reveal during their meetings with clients. Many people who have gone through a divorce wish their attorney had been more forthcoming and knowledgeable about the process.

Major problems can occur when payments are missed. The missed payments start showing up on both spouse's credit reports, and both of their credit scores begin to suffer. And, if the late payments start becoming of the more severe variety, the lender can begin collection actions against both parties, regardless of what the judge said.

So, what happens, for example, if I have a joint car loan with my ex-spouse and the judge says my ex gets the car and that she has to make the payments...but she doesn't? The car will eventually get repossessed and a record of that will show up on both of our credit reports, trashing both of our scores for up to seven years, fair or not.

This is one of those unexpected things that nobody thinks about until it's too late. I've spoken to thousands of women and men who went through a divorce and ended up destroying their credit at the same time, without even realizing what they were doing. Now, not only do they have to recover from the trauma of going through the divorce, but they also have to figure out how to rebuild their credit reports and credit scores.

So how can I avoid this?

First off, each spouse should establish their own credit while they are single and continue to do so while they are married. This doesn't mean that you should avoid co-applying for credit. It means that you should also have your own accounts with banks, retails stores, cell phone companies, gasoline companies, auto lenders, or anywhere else that will help you establish credit. Maintaining credit independence is a good thing.

You're going to need to jointly apply for some of your more expensive purchases like homes and cars because you might need both incomes to qualify for the loan. But remember: If you apply jointly, you and your spouse are both on the hook for the payment. For the big-ticket items, both of you should apply. However, for the small stuff like credit cards or cellular services, one applicant is plenty.

One of the mistakes people make when they get married is thinking they don't need to apply for and manage their own credit because they have their spouse's credit to fall back on. **This is a much bigger problem for women than it is for men.** Spouses who neglect to establish or maintain existing credit are typically women.

What they don't realize is that an individual's credit report will eventually become outdated, which can hurt credit scores. Simply closing all of your accounts and not opening any more new accounts will lead to what's referred to as a "stagnant" credit report. That's not good.

The reason it's not good is that about half of the people who get married will also get divorced. If you've allowed your credit reports to become stagnant, you're going to have a very difficult time getting credit at competitive rates if you try to apply as a newly single person. It's almost as if you never existed and are now starting over from scratch.

It's not as if you're a bad credit risk. Rather, since all of your personal accounts are all closed or have long since disappeared from your credit reports, you seem to be new to credit altogether. This is such a shame because you could have established credit when you were married.

I almost made this mistake myself. When I got married, I chose to close down all of my gasoline credit cards and both of my bank credit cards. My wife had all of the really good credit cards with high limits and rewards programs so I just had my name added to her accounts. If I had left things like that and hadn't established any new credit in my name, my credit reports would have eventually ceased to exist and my credit scores would have followed, thus making it impossible for me to establish any new credit without jumping through major hoops.

Thankfully, I did establish new accounts in my name in addition to my jointly held accounts, so my credit reports and scores are just fine. But if I didn't know about credit scoring through my industry experience, I could have made a horrible mistake. Unfortunately, millions of people make that mistake every year when they get married and it leads to problems if they get divorced.

So what do I do if I've already made that mistake?

This is going to sound a little strange, but if you know that you are going to be filing for divorce, you should prepare your credit well before you file. This is not something your divorce attorney will, can, or should do for you. This is something you have to do on your own.

If you haven't yet established credit in your own name, it's time to open a few accounts. The easiest accounts to get are retail store credit cards and secured credit cards. Open two or three, but that's about it. Use them conservatively and pay them off at the end of each month. Remember, we're not trying to get you into debt. We're simply trying to knock the dust off of your credit files by adding new accounts.

If you only have joint accounts with your soon-to-be ex-spouse, the task is going to be much more difficult. Your goal is to turn joint accounts into individual accounts, so that it will be easier for the divorce court to split up your financial responsibilities – you keep your accounts, your spouse keeps his or hers. But before you make any changes to your jointly held accounts, you need your spouse's permission. That means you're going to have to let the cat out the bag.

Your first focus should be on the plastic. That's because people most often miss payments on credit card accounts. Your ex-spouse is less likely to miss a payment on a home or car loan out of fear of foreclosure or repossession. Most people will bend over backward to keep a roof over their heads and wheels under their feet.

Besides, if you have joint credit on a mortgage or a car loan, it's going to be much more difficult to convert either of those to individual accounts. The bank will want just one person to refinance the loan in his or her name. That may not be possible if the person's individual salary isn't enough to qualify for the loan. In cases like these, it will probably be easier to sell the house and the cars, split the proceeds, and move on. That way, you're guaranteed not to have any credit damages caused by an irresponsible or vengeful ex-spouse.

Start planning ahead as much as possible. Get as much of this done before the divorce starts getting ugly. Once the problems start, you and your soon-to-be ex-spouse will have a harder time thinking logically. You want to start this process at least 6-12 months before you file, maybe even longer.

If you can successfully convert all of your joint credit into individual credit, your ex-spouse won't be able to hurt your credit or credit scores by missing payments after the divorce is finalized. It's a lot of work on the front end of the divorce, but it will save you seven to ten years of credit-related headaches on the back end.

If you have to find a job after your divorce, you should be aware of the fact that employers can and will use your credit reports to determine whether or not you are a good fit. That means if you don't take the time to properly address your credit before the divorce, you might not only have credit and insurance troubles. You might find it impossible to get a job, too. It need not be said these are potentially huge problems that should be taken very seriously.

Chapter 5

Bankruptcy and Credit Counseling

I'm sure you've all heard the term *bankruptcy*. Essentially it means that you've determined you cannot pay your bills any longer and must ask for legal help with your debt. The help that you get via a bankruptcy is called a "discharge." Bankruptcy is the legal way that some consumers can be excused (or discharged) from paying some or all of their debts. It's a process that involves lawyers, a judge, and the court system.

There are two main types of bankruptcy that you can file. They are:

Chapter 13

This is commonly referred to as a "Wage Earner Plan." In this type of bankruptcy, you, the consumer, will continue to make payments to the court or a trustee of the court, which are then dispersed to your creditors. The creditors get much less than they are owed but at least they get something. Chapter 13 bankruptcies will remain on your credit reports for seven years from the discharge date or a maximum of ten years. And since it takes roughly three to five years to discharge Chapter 13 bankruptcies, you can bet that if you file a chapter

13 it will be on your credit reports for ten full years.

Chapter 7

This type of bankruptcy discharges all of the debt that you're allowed to discharge, meaning you don't have to make any more payments. Under the new bankruptcy laws, you have to qualify to be able to file for this type of bankruptcy. If you make too much money compared to others that live in your state, you'll be forced to file a Chapter 13 bankruptcy and make some sort of payment to the court-assigned trustee. Chapter 7 bankruptcies will remain on your credit reports for ten years from the date filed.

Now that we have a very basic level of understanding of what a bankruptcy is, let's talk about the effect filing for bankruptcy will have on your credit. Some people think that it's the absolute worst thing you can do to your credit. That's not really the case. Filing for bankruptcy just prolongs the effect of an already bad credit report and already low credit scores.

You see, most people who file for bankruptcy already have significant payment problems and excessive debt that is already reflected on their credit reports. As such, their scores are already much lower than they once were. The credit damage incurred through late payments, collections and increasing debt eventually culminates with the coup de gráce: the bankruptcy filing. This is what I call the "bankruptcy crescendo effect."

So, while bankruptcy doesn't normally add significantly more damage to your credit scores, it does guarantee that your scores will continue to suffer for the next ten years, even after the accounts that were discharged by the bankruptcy are long gone from your credit reports. Remember, the accounts can only stay on your reports for seven years, while the record of your bankruptcy can remain on your file for at *least* seven and probably ten years.

It's safe to say that people who have good credit aren't the ones filing for bankruptcy. But if they did, their scores would tank overnight. Credit scores are like water; they will take the path of least resistance. If your scores are already low, another negative item will have less of an overall effect than the first negative item to hit your reports. At that point, you would have had more to lose. But by the time you file for bankruptcy, if you choose to do so, your scores will have already reached their low point.

What makes bankruptcy such a shame is that the people filing for it aren't just those who mismanage their credit. If you took a survey of people who filed for bankruptcy, you'd hear all sorts of explanations. Some people would have had to file because they lost their jobs. Others would have filed due to a divorce, a failed business venture, or savings that had been wiped out by medical expenses. And yes, there are those who file for bankruptcy simply because they ran up too much debt and could no longer handle it. But don't think that a majority of people file because they're bad credit managers. That couldn't be further from the truth.

So you're probably wondering, is there an alternative to bankruptcy? For some people there is, but for others bankruptcy remains the best option. One alternative is a Debt Management Plan (or DMP) offered by a reputable credit counseling service such as any member of the National Foundation for Credit Counseling (www.nfcc.org). A DMP allows the consumer to pay a monthly amount to the counseling agency, which is then disbursed to your creditors. Normally the counseling agency can negotiate lower interest rates or even a waiver for a period of time, thus making it easier to pay off your balances faster than you could have on your own.

Completing a DMP can take several years. The advantage is that it does not lower your credit scores like a bankruptcy would. That said, most creditors will shy away from doing business with you nevertheless. They do not want to grant you credit and have you add them to the plan. So, while you are in the plan it might be wise to avoid applying for credit.

Chapter 6

How Do I Earn a Great Credit Report and Great Credit Scores?

D id some of you jump forward directly to this chapter? I can't blame you if you did. This is why you paid the price of admission, isn't it? As you've no doubt already figured out, our credit scores are a direct reflection of the information found in our credit reports. If you don't have great credit reports, you're not going to have great credit scores. It's that simple.

But, there's a dilemma. Since we are not taught how to properly establish the right kinds of credit, we are usually forced to retrofit our existing credit reports so that we score well, rather than establish solid credit from the beginning. In a perfect world, we'd all get an in-depth class on how to build our credit reports before we opened our first credit account. That way, we could open the right types of accounts with the right lenders and make our lives much simpler.

Since we don't live in this perfect credit world, we have to play the cards we've dealt ourselves in the years we've been establishing credit. That's not as bad as it sounds. The longer you've had credit, the easier it is to make small changes and earn better scores. This is a process that I call "Credit Optimization."

Here are what I consider to be the most important rules to follow when you choose to go through Credit Optimization. It works whether you are establishing or re-establishing credit.

Rule 1: Understand the value of time

The older your credit file, the more stable it is. That's not only a common sense observation but also a statistical fact. Consumers that have older credit histories tend to be better credit risks and will earn more points simply because of the age of their credit reports than those consumers with younger credit histories. Also, the older your credit file, the less your credit scores will fluctuate when you open new accounts or run up large balances for a short period of time.

The way the age of your credit history is determined or "dated" is pretty simple. Credit scoring models will look at all of the accounts on your credit reports and take the one with the oldest "date opened" and use that as your credit report's date of birth. A second factor looks at every single account on your individual credit reports and comes up with an average age based upon how old each of the accounts is.

If I have two accounts on one of my credit reports and the older of the two was opened 10 years ago, my credit report is 10 years old. If the second account was opened 5 years ago, my credit report's average age is 7.5 years. It's that simple. The older those dates are, the better they are for your credit score.

Now that you know this, it should be very clear to you why it's important to **never try to get old, good accounts off of your credit reports simply because they're old or closed.** There's a huge credit myth floating around that consumers should try and get old accounts removed from their credit reports. That could be a disaster, especially if you're successful in getting them removed.

By removing old accounts, you are making your credit report look younger. And younger credit reports equate to you being a higher-risk consumer. It's going to be harder for you to earn a great score if you get old accounts removed. I think that myth grew out of articles which talked about how you should try to get old negative accounts removed. That would make more sense.

Here's the bottom line on trying to get accounts removed. Negative information on your credit reports can only stay on as long as the law allows. In most instances, that can't be any longer than seven to ten years, depending on the type of item. So, the law is going to require that the credit reporting agencies clean off the old, negative account/s for you. You don't need to do a thing except wait.

The good accounts can stay on indefinitely, and you want them there indefinitely. I always use this analogy when advising people who are trying to get old, good information removed:

If you made straight A's in high school or graduated from college with a 4.0 grade point average, would you ever want that history to go away? Of course you wouldn't. It's the same thing with good credit. Why in the world would you ever want your history of solid credit management removed? There is no reason, so don't try. It can only hurt you.

These "age" related factors, while important to an overall healthy credit report and credit scores, are not the most important factors in determining your score. They are what I refer to as "side dishes." They may add a nice touch to your meal, but they're not the reason you order a meal. You order because of the steak! So let's talk about one of the steak categories.

Rule 2: Ask yourself, "Exactly how much is this going to cost me?"

You should become very familiar with this statement: "A great credit report is not necessarily a credit report that doesn't have late payments." Think about that for a moment, a great credit report is NOT necessarily a credit report that doesn't have late payments. Or you can say it this way...a bad credit report isn't always a credit report with late payments on it. To assume that simply managing to pay your bills on time will lead to a great credit report and great credit scores would be incorrect.

Many people simply don't know that their amount of debt is a huge factor in determining their credit scores. Here's why: **People who have a lot of debt pose a greater credit risk than people with less debt**. In fact, your amount of debt is the second most important factor in your credit scores. You can lose a lot of credit score points if you don't do well in the debt category.

The people who find this out the hard way are the folks who are making minimum payments on their credit cards. Yes, they are paying their bills and making their payments on time. This certainly helps. But, by making only the minimum payments, their debt never really decreases enough to earn them all of the credit score points they could be earning. And at the same time, they are probably still making purchases on the credit cards, so their balances continue to increase month after month. At the very least their balances are not decreasing.

Please become familiar with the term "revolving utilization." It is the amount of your credit card's credit limits that you are currently using as a balance. So, if you have a credit card with a $1,000 credit limit and a balance of $500, your revolving utilization on that credit card is 50% because you are using up half of that card's available credit limit. This is a measurement that the credit scoring models take whenever your credit score is calculated. And, it's calculated at an aggregate credit report level (all of your open credit cards together) and at the individual level (each card's utilization is calculated separately as well).

The higher the percentages, the more difficult it will be to earn a great credit score. If the category about age was a "side dish," this category is definitely part of your main course. It is extremely important to know what your revolving utilization percentage is at all times. If you can control it and keep it low, your scores will be much better.

Most people focus on paying their bills on time and pay very little attention to their utilization. The truth is that you can lose more points by having a high utilization than you can by missing payments. That's right. A high utilization can damage your credit scores more than some late payments. And the worst part about this one is that consumers are almost always told, "As long as your utilization is below 50% your scores will be fine."

This is simply incorrect – another myth. As the percentage increases, the amount of credit score points you can earn decreases. So, 50% is better than 60% but it's not as good as 40%. Consumers who simply think that if they can use half of their credit limits and still score well are mistaken. Nothing magical happens at 50%.

The optimal percentage is less than 10%. That means if you have a credit card with a $1000 credit limit, you should ideally use no more than $100 of it at any given time. I recognize that this significantly reduces the value of having a credit card if you can only use 10% of the credit limit. The good news is that since this is also an aggregate measurement (all of your cards measured as one) you can play around with the cards you use and those that you don't use and keep your overall utilization around 10%.

Here's a real example of how I use multiple cards to keep my overall utilization low. I have five credit cards. If you add up their credit limits, the total is $94,000. In order for me to maintain utilization under 10% I can't charge more than $9,400 in any month. This works out just fine because I rarely, if ever, have a need to charge more than that amount. If I ever do, it's for work-related expenses and I pay the balance off when I get my expenses reimbursed. I have assured myself of always getting the lion's share of the points from the debt category by strategically setting up my credit cards. It's my own little utilization insurance policy.

The best thing for you to do is take a look at your credit reports and determine what your total credit limits and total balances are. Call it a "utilization diagnostic." Then you will be able to calculate your total utilization and see where you need to cut back in order to maintain 10%. This may require you to increase the credit limits on a few of your cards or even open a new card. The whole utilization challenge is really nothing more than a math problem. You're just trying to play with the numbers to ensure that you're getting the most possible credit score points.

Rule 3: Shop till you and your credit scores drop

Shopping for credit is harmless, right? You might be surprised to learn that simply applying for credit can hurt your credit reports and lower your credit scores. In some cases, it can lower your scores significantly, to the point where you could be approved at less than the best interest rates or even declined for credit altogether.

Every time you apply for credit, the lender will almost certainly pull at least one, and possibly all three of, your credit reports. Each time this happens, the credit reporting agencies are required to keep a record of who pulled your reports and on what date. This record is commonly referred to as an "inquiry" or "credit inquiry." These inquiries can remain on your credit reports for up to two years.

This is one of the more frustrating aspects of credit scoring. The requirement of the credit bureaus to keep a record of who pulled your credit reports and on what dates was put into place many years ago for your benefit. It's there to protect you by always providing a record of who is looking at your credit reports and scores.

Unfortunately, those inquiries have become somewhat of an Achilles' heel for all of us who care about our credit scores. You see, each time your credit is pulled and an inquiry is posted, your credit scores can go down. The reason they can go down is that it's been statistically proven that consumers who are acquiring more credit are a higher risk of missing payments than consumers who are not. That means for every inquiry you have, your credit scores could go down.

There are several situations that we all need to be aware of in order to reduce (or even eliminate) the negative impact of inquiries on our credit scores. They are:

- During the holiday season – Whenever we go shopping at the malls during the holiday season we are offered discounts for signing up for store credit cards. On the surface these sound like a good deal. If we can save 10% of our purchase, that could translate to $10, $20 or even more. My advice is **Don't Do It!!** You'll only hurt yourself in the long run. Why? Each one of those store card applications you fill out will result in an inquiry on your credit report. To make matters worse, retail store inquiries are among the worst kind for your scores.

- At kiosks at sporting events or at the airport – Those of us who attend sporting events or travel via airports know that you can't walk down the aisles without some sort of offer for a free shirt, hat, coffee mug or some other freebie in exchange for signing up for a credit card. While that free NASCAR t-shirt might be really tempting, you should avoid it like the plague. Why? Each one of those free gifts will result in an inquiry on your credit report by the credit card company. Like retail store inquiries, credit card inquiries are among the worst kind for your scores.

Each of the above mentioned inquires can lower your credit scores.

And the more of them you have, the more your scores could suffer. Inquiries can harm credit scores for a full twelve months. That means if you opened a store card at The Gap in December, that inquiry is likely to lower your credit score until the following December. Is that worth 10% off of your purchase? It certainly is not.

Remember, lenders will use our credit reports and scores to determine the interest rates we pay on everything from credit cards to car loans to mortgages. You could cost yourself thousands of dollars if you lower your scores simply by saving a few bucks on some clothes or by falling for the free T-shirt trick at a football game. Here's an example…

Scenario #1
Brad goes to a NASCAR race and is offered a free duffle bag if he will sign up for a credit card. Not knowing the damage it could cause, Brad happily signs up and walks away a happy man with duffle bag in tow.

Seven months later, Brad applies to refinance his home loan of $235,000. He is approved, but the rate he is offered is higher than he expected because of his credit scores. After some research, he finds out that the reason his scores are not up to snuff is because of the inquiry the credit card company caused when they ran his credit application and pulled his credit report. Since the mortgage interest rates are rising at the time, Brad decides to take their less than great offer and ends up with a payment of $2,100.

*Image used with the permission of Brad Julian.

Scenario #2

Brad goes to a NASCAR race and politely declines the offer for the free duffle bag. Seven months later, Brad applies and refinances his home loan at the best interest rate currently available. He gets the lender's best rate partially because of his excellent credit scores. His monthly payment is $1,750, a full $350 less than it would have been in Scenario #1. Please keep this in mind the next time you are offered a discount or a freebie in exchange for applying for a credit or retail store card. NEVER trade access to your credit reports and scores for something as invaluable as a T-shirt, coffee mug, or duffle bag.

Inquiries are not a score-killer like excessive debt or missing payments are, but they are worth enough that even a few of them can wreak havoc to even the best scores. In the Master's Level chapter, we'll discuss the optimal way to shop for credit so that you can minimize the negative impact to your scores. There is a very easy way to shop strategically so that your scores will remain relatively unaffected.

Rule 4: Evaluate what KIND of credit you have

Did you know that the type of credit you use has an impact to your score? Have you ever thought about this when you're in the process of opening new accounts? Did you think about this when you first started establishing credit? Don't worry; nobody else did either.

One of the more frustrating things about credit scores is that there is no single piece of advice from this category I can give that will allow every one of you readers to earn the maximum number of score points. What's good for me may not be good for you, and vice versa. It's impossible to give you advice on how to perform perfectly in this category.

But, there are some general rules that do apply to all of us. We'll focus on those.

Do not use finance companies under any circumstances.

A finance company is a lender that targets high-risk consumers. Their loan products are designed to protect them in case their customers decide that they don't want to pay. Basically, they charge all of their customers very high interest rates and have very restrictive credit terms designed to keep tight control over the money that people have borrowed from them.

Besides high interest rates and poor treatment, finance companies have another nasty byproduct. Simply having them on your credit reports can lower your credit scores even if you pay them on time and have very low balances. That's right. You can be doing everything right and still suffer simply because you're doing business with them.

Consumers who have finance company accounts on their credit reports pose a higher credit risk than those who do not. That's a statistical fact. And the worst part about them is that once they're on your credit reports, it's next to impossible to get them off.

And besides, you may not want them to come off anyway. That finance company account could be helping the "age" of your credit report and also be keeping your utilization low if it's a credit card with a low balance. The tradeoff of having it removed could actually lower your score. If you get to this stage, it becomes very frustrating because you're damned if you do and damned if you don't.

This is perhaps the best example of where some sort of education on the subject of establishing credit would have come in handy. In this case, what you don't know can definitely hurt your credit scores.

So you vow to avoid finance companies at all costs. Good for you... but can you really do it?

Imagine walking into a furniture store and buying an expensive bedroom suite. It's something that many of us have done or will do. The salesperson will almost certainly offer you some sort of incentive to finance the purchase such as "same as cash" or a payment deferment of several months or even years. These offers also sound great on the surface but can negatively affect your credit. That's because many of the large furniture and electronics retailers do not have their own banks and instead partner with a finance company in order to make these offers to consumers. So, by taking advantage of a special offer to finance a new television set or furniture, you may accidentally establish credit with a finance company.

Before you sign anything, always read the credit agreement. The fine print will let you know who their lending partner is and help you determine whether or not you should avoid them.

It's important that you buy a house.

It's important not only for the direct financial benefits – tax deduction, for example, or the fact that a home is usually an appreciating asset. Home ownership is also important because it equates to stability. And, stability equates to low credit risk.

Of course, the only way for any credit score to account for your mortgage is for the mortgage to be listed as an account on your credit reports. Once it's there, you will benefit. And, the beauty is that as long as it's on your credit report you'll always benefit, regardless of whether you even live in the house.

Be sure that you're getting credit for your good credit.

As I mentioned, the only way your credit score will benefit from the fact that you have a mortgage is if the credit scoring models know about it through your credit reports. Since credit reporting is a voluntary act that your lenders may or may not participate in, you need to know if your excellent credit management is going to waste. There is no rule or law that forces lenders to report your accounts to the credit reporting agencies. And, there's no rule or law that says if a lender reports to one credit reporting agency, it must also report to any of the other credit reporting agencies. In fact, there are many lenders who will choose to only report to one or two of the three. For the most part this isn't a big deal. If you have nothing but good accounts that have respectable balances then some record of them will likely be on all three of your credit reports. Where it becomes a problem is when the consumer is trying to establish new credit accounts or trying to rebuild their credit.

In these situations, consumers need as much good credit on their credit reports as they can get. If their lenders aren't telling everyone about the good credit that's already established, it will take them longer to establish three credit reports that are worthy of excellent credit scores. It's that simple.

Before applying for a loan, especially a mortgage, ask the lender to tell you which of the credit reporting agencies they will be sending your account information to. If they tell you that they report to all three then you're fine. If they only report to one or two of them, you have to decide whether or not the omission is going to hurt you. If so, you may consider a different lender.

Rule 5: Pay your bills on time!

Because the common sense of this rule is so obvious you might wonder who needs to buy a book about credit scoring that tells you to pay your bills when they are due. Although this book's focus is on sharing information that is NOT common sense, I'd be drummed out of the credit-scoring sewing circles if I didn't talk about the importance of timely payments. The first thing that you need to understand is that it doesn't matter how many days you're late, and it doesn't matter how much you owe on past due accounts. What really mat-

> *"A check is nothing more than a commitment to pay someone else an amount of money."*

ters is what your creditors tell the credit bureaus about your tardiness. Did you get that? It only matters what your lenders tell the credit bureaus about your tardiness.

Credit scores are very smart, sophisticated programs. They are also very limited because they only take into account what shows up on your credit reports. And, if you are 6 months past due with your credit card company and they don't tell any of the credit bureaus about it…then your scores won't suffer one bit. What I'm telling you is that not all lenders will nail you to the wall just because you miss a payment by a few days. But, some of them will report your account as being late even if you are late by only one day. You just never know. It's completely up to them when they will start telling the world about your late payments.

Late payments are only the beginning of what can hurt you from this category. Think about what happens to one of your accounts if you simply stop making your payments. The lender will have its representatives call you and then send you letters, hoping that this will convince you to send them a check. They'll eventually tell the credit bureaus about your unwillingness to pay. That's where the trouble really begins.

After a few months of unsuccessful attempts to get you to pay, they'll send the account to their internal collection team. These pleasant folks are trained to collect debts that people are unwilling to pay. If they're unsuccessful, the lender will eventually give up and "charge off" the account. That means the lender has essentially given up and wants to get the debt off of its taxable books. When the lender charges off the account, it will probably sell the debt or consign it to an outside collection agency that will also try to collect from you. And if worse comes to worse, the lender might even repossess your car (if it was a car loan) or foreclose on your home (if it was a home loan) or even sue you.

This whole process might take three to six months, and all the while the credit reporting agencies are getting detailed updates about all of it. Eventually, your lenders might even start suing you, the IRS will start filing tax liens against you, and then when it seems as if it could get no worse, you may have to go out and file for bankruptcy. This ascending level of derogatory events will all be on your credit reports, destroying your credit scores and any chance you have at getting credit or insurance at decent rates for between seven and ten years.

As you can see, on top of being the most common sense advice, it is also the most important rule.

Chapter 7

Your Rights

One of the things that all of the books I've read about credit have in common is they all have incredibly boring chapters about the laws that govern the use of credit reports and credit scores. Most of them practically require a law degree to understand because they quote the text of the law as written rather than interpret it so that you and I can understand it. Don't worry – what follows is easy to digest.

Federal Law

When it comes to credit, it pretty much begins and ends with the Fair Credit Reporting Act (FCRA). The FCRA is basically written like any other law. I say that because it's about twice as long as it needs to be. I'm of the opinion that consumers only need to be familiar with the following three most important sections of the FCRA:

1. Permissible Purpose

This is the section that says who is allowed to have access to your credit reports and why. A person or company cannot access your credit information if they don't satisfy one of the following criteria.

By the way, if your report is pulled for any of the following reasons, an inquiry will be posted on your credit report, which you may or may not ever see.

The following are purposes for which a credit report may be obtained:

⏺ *At your request* – If you want to see a copy of your own credit reports, you have the right to get them, for free in many cases.

⏺ *In response to a court order* – Your credit reports can be subpoenaed by the courts or by an attorney representing you or defending someone that you are suing. This is very common in cases where consumers are suing lenders accusing them of damaging their credit reports by reporting incorrect information.

⏺ *For the purposes of determining employment eligibility* – This one really gets people steamed. When you apply for a job, your prospective employer has the right to pull your credit reports and use them to determine whether or not you're a good candidate. And while the law doesn't allow an employer to use a credit report as the sole reason to deny someone a job, I've spoken to enough Human Resources people off the record to know that they are certainly a very important factor in many cases.

In many cases, credit is pulled when the applicant has access to sensitive information or a cash drawer. Think about it…do you really want to put someone who has crushing debt in front of a cash drawer at a bank? That's awfully tempting.

⏺ *For insurance underwriting* – This one is by far the most controversial. Insurance companies can use your credit reports (and insurance credit scores) to determine whether or not they want to insure your house or car and how much your premiums will be. Consumer groups really hate this one because they argue that there is no correlation between credit management and insurance risk.

•• ***To grant credit, review an account, or collect a debt*** – This is the most popular. This "reason to pull credit" results in hundreds of millions of credit reports being pulled each year. Basically, this one gives a lender permission to pull your credit report if you apply for a loan. It also gives them the right to review your credit report periodically while you have an existing account with them. And, if you stop making your payments, they can pull your credit reports for the purpose of trying to collect the debt.

•• ***Child support related*** – Child support agencies can pull credit reports to determine an individual's ability to pay child support.

2. FACTA (FACT ACT)

FACTA, the Fair and Accurate Credit Transactions Act of 2003, is part of the Fair Credit Reporting Act. This relatively recent change to the FCRA gives everyone in the country the right to get a free copy of their various "consumer reports" once a year from any agency that stores them.

This means that every one of us can get our credit reports from Equifax, Experian, TransUnion and any other new credit reporting agencies once a year at no cost. Also, you can get a copy of the report that is stored by a company called ChoicePoint. They store and sell your insurance claim information to insurance companies. Basically, any report that is used by another party to "evaluate" you is addressed in FACTA and you are entitled to a free copy of it each year.

There are several ways to get your free reports. You can claim them online at www.annualcreditreport.com or you can request them by phone at 1-877-322-8228. If neither of those options is your cup of tea then you can write and request your reports. The address is:

Annual Credit Report Request Service
PO Box 105283
Atlanta, GA 30348-5283

3. Dispute Resolution

The Fair Credit Reporting Act also sets the rules for when you have a dispute over something on your credit reports. We all have the right to dispute anything that we disagree with that's on our credit reports. Whether or not we'll be successful in changing anything is a different story.

The FCRA says that if we feel something is incomplete or incorrect we can challenge the information. And, the credit reporting agencies have 30 days from the day they were notified of the dispute to validate whether or not the item is being reporting correctly. If it's verified as being accurate, it stays. If the evaluation determines the item is incorrect, it is either removed or changed so that it is being reported correctly. It's that simple.

But consumers need to be very careful when disputing information on their credit files. I point this out because of a common tactic used by credit repair companies, which are sometimes hired by people whose credit scores are low. As explained in more detail in Chapter 8, they will send letters of dispute over and over to the credit bureaus on behalf of their clients to dispute the negative listings on their credit reports, even if those listings are accurate. The credit repair companies are hoping that eventually the credit bureaus will be unable to verify the information in the allotted 30 day time period and therefore they will have to remove it. However, if a credit bureau has determined the disputes are frivolous, they do not have to verify it over and over again, which means that you may have difficulty with legitimate disputes in the future.

State Disclosure Rights

In addition to the FACTA annual freebies I talked about earlier, you could also be eligible for free credit reports based upon where you live. Certain states have laws that guarantee their residents access to free reports. These laws can change, but as of this writing the list is as follows:

Colorado:	1 free per calendar year
Georgia:	2 free per calendar year
Maine:	1 free every 12 months
Maryland:	1 free every 12 months
Massachusetts:	1 free per calendar year
New Jersey:	1 free every 12 months
Vermont:	1 free every 12 months

Other rules for free reports:

There are also rules that guarantee free credit reports:

- *If you are unemployed and will search for a job in the next 60 days.*
- *If you are on public assistance, like welfare.*
- *If you believe you've been the victim of fraud.*
- *If you've been denied credit, insurance, or employment in the past 60 days.*

If you fall into any of the categories listed above, you are entitled to 1 free copy of your credit report every 12 months.

Chapter 8

Credit Repair and Credit Clinics

T his is a fun chapter. It's all about credit repair and how credit repair organizations (a.k.a. Credit Clinics or Credit Doctors) operate. First things first: let's define exactly what credit repair is. Credit repair is the process whereby you or someone acting on your behalf goes to the credit reporting agencies and attempts to get information removed from your credit reports. And, just to be crystal clear...all of the information I share in this chapter I learned while I was working for Equifax in the early and late 1990's.

The vast majority of the time, the information that is under attack is negative...and 100% accurate. The goal of the credit repair company is to get negative information removed from your credit reports so that your credit scores will be higher and lenders and insurance companies will think you are a lower risk than you really are. As you've no doubt already figured, credit repair isn't really an ethical endeavor. Getting legitimately incorrect information removed from your credit reports is not credit repair. Don't get the two confused.

The companies that sell credit repair services generally charge an up-front set up fee and a reoccurring monthly fee to do their work. Normally that fee ranges from $39 per month all the way up to $89 per month. The real question about credit repair companies is: "Exactly what are they doing for their fee?"

Here's where it gets really slimy. What these companies are doing is sending letters to the credit bureaus as if they were you. That's right, most of these companies ask you to sign some sort of limited power of attorney granting them the ability to sign your name to a letter. The letters they send to the credit reporting agencies are signed in your name, but really are written and sent by them.

These letters dispute anything that is negative, including late payments, liens, charge offs, collections, and even bankruptcies. Their disputes range from something as simple as "Those accounts are not mine" all the way to "I was the victim of identity theft and that's where that account came from." What all of their disputes have in common is that they are all disputing items that are probably 100% accurate.

That begs the following question: Should they really be called "credit repair" companies? When I think of the word "repair," I think of fixing something that's broken. In this case, they are trying to fix something that you just don't want: your bad credit. It's certainly not broken.

"You can do the same thing they do for the cost of a stamp, envelope and a piece of paper."

These companies will get copies of your credit reports from you, identify all of the negative items, and then simply send dispute letters to the credit bureaus trying to get items removed from your credit reports. But guess what? You can do the exact same thing yourself. And, you can do it for the cost of a stamp and an envelope.

What are they trying to do?

Credit repair organizations are trying to play what's referred to in the credit repair world as "the 30 day game." In the "Your Rights" chapter, we talk about how credit-reporting agencies have 30 days to perform an investigation on any items that you dispute. If the item is not verified within 30 days, the credit bureaus have to either remove it or change it in your favor. The credit repair companies are well aware of this.

They will send letters to the credit bureaus and then, after the bureaus complete their investigations, they will send another round of letters re-disputing any negative items that came back as "verified correct." What they are hoping is that at some point the ball gets dropped and the lender or courthouse won't verify the account again within the next 30 day time frame. If it comes back as "verified correct" again, then they'll send another round of dispute letters, and so on and so forth. That's what you get for your monthly fee.

What do the credit reporting agencies do about this?

The credit reporting agencies all have special units that are always on the look out for credit clinic disputes. If they determine that your dispute is being handled by a credit repair organization and the disputes that are being submitted on your behalf are bogus, then they can, by law, ignore any subsequent requests as being "frivolous." If your credit file is flagged as being involved with a credit repair organization, you're going to have a very difficult time getting anything removed from your credit files in the future.

Credit clinic letters used to be very easy to identify. They would all quote section 611 from the Fair Credit Reporting Act (procedures in case of consumer disputes) and were all form letters. They would also send all of their dispute letters from the same post office location. So, if a consumer lived in New York but his dispute letter had a Houston, Texas postmark, the discrepancy would set off a red flag to the credit bureaus.

Credit clinics would also send their letters out in large batches from the same post office. So, when they showed up at the credit bureaus they would be in a large stack…letters from consumers living all around the country, all sent from the same city, all the same form letter, quoting the same section of the Fair Credit Reporting Act. The credit bureaus picked those out easily.

Once the credit bureaus identified a letter as being from a credit clinic, they sent a letter directly to the consumer telling them that hiring a company to dispute their credit reports was a waste of money since they could submit legitimate disputes themselves for free. To combat this, the credit clinics would tell their clients, "Don't even open the letters that the credit bureaus send you…just drop them in an envelope and send them to us and we'll deal with them." This would prevent consumers from seeing that they could submit disputes on their own for free.

How have credit clinics evolved?

Today, the credit clinics have become much more sophisticated than they use to be in the past. They know that the credit bureaus are on to them and are looking out for their letters. So, as any company does…the credit clinics have had to change how they do business in order to stay in business.

Today's credit clinics have hired insiders who currently work at the credit bureaus in positions to change credit information. For a fee, they will change or delete information from the credit reports of the credit clinic's customers. This is highly illegal. When these insiders get caught, as they all eventually do, they are normally prosecuted.

Credit clinics have also learned that it's much more efficient for them to get the credit reports directly from the credit bureaus themselves rather then depend on their clients to request their own reports and mail them the paper copies once they show up in the mail. So, many credit clinics have created fake lenders and applied for and been granted direct access to the credit bureau's databases. This is a willful violation of the Fair Credit Reporting Act.

Fake mortgage companies are a favorite choice of credit clinics since mortgage lenders always pull all three of your credit reports when you apply. This way, the credit clinics can pull all three of your credit reports without suspicion. What's so surprising is that the credit bureaus do very little to validate that the companies they do business with are legitimate when they apply, and remain legitimate throughout their relationship. Credit clinics know this and have exploited it.

Having direct access to the credit bureau's databases is great for their business. It's more efficient for them to determine what to dispute because they have real time access to your credit reports. In fact, it's easier for them to get your credit reports than it is for you to get your own credit reports.

The one drawback to the fake lender strategy is that whenever they pull your credit reports, they leave behind a breadcrumb called an inquiry. Remember what an inquiry is? It's a record of who pulled your credit reports and on what date. The inquiries posted by the fake lenders can lower your credit scores.

But all of this credit report stuff still doesn't address the process of the generating and mailing of dispute letters. Unfortunately for the credit bureaus, the credit repair agencies have figured out a way around that little hurdle as well. It's a mixture of new and old school technology.

To get around the postmark issues, the credit clinics now use a modified version of something called drop shipping. They still mail the dispute letter to the credit bureaus, but now they will actually send it from the city you live in. How they do it is pretty easy. They will sign up for an account with a local mail service, send your letter there, and pay them to drop it in the mail. That way it gets a local postmark and doesn't show any red flags at the credit bureaus.

Is this legal?

That's the million-dollar question. There's a law that governs how credit repair organizations do business. It's called the Credit Repair Organizations Act (CROA). It doesn't prohibit companies from doing credit repair, but it does say how they have to do it. One of the CROA rules is that the companies that perform credit repair cannot take an up-front fee for their work. They are only allowed to charge you once the work has been completed. The question is: Are they charging you for simply sending letters month after month, or are they charging you for actually getting things removed from your credit reports? It's a gray area for sure. Certainly, setting up fake lenders and pulling credit reports are violations of the Fair Credit Reporting Act. There are also a number of settled and pending cases for violations of CROA.

Many credit repair organizations are formed as law firms that offer credit repair as part of their "legal services." Being a law firm exempts their credit repair entities from CROA regulations but opens up a new can of worms: are they really legitimate law firms? Only lawyers can own a law firm, so a credit clinic that calls itself a law firm but is owned by non-lawyers is not a legitimate law firm. Even if the firm is owned by lawyers, the law firm must practice other types of law, not only credit repair services, in order to perform these services without CROA regulation.

The bottom line: If you choose to inundate the credit bureaus with letters disputing accurate information, that's certainly your choice. But, paying someone to do the exact same thing seems foolish. Their letters won't work any better than your letters would.

Chapter 9
Credit and Insurance

Nothing infuriates consumers and consumer advocates more than this fact: insurance companies use your credit reports and credit scores to determine what insurance you qualify for and at what rates. And guess what? I totally agree with the insurance companies. They should be able to use your credit data to determine your insurability. Here's why:

First and foremost, it's completely legal for insurance companies to use your credit reports. The Fair Credit Reporting Act specifically says that your credit reports can be used "in connection with the underwriting of insurance." No arguments there. Insurance companies are in the business of making money, and the only way they can make money is if you pay them more (premiums) than they pay out on your behalf (claims). So, insurance companies are really using your credit information to determine whether or not you're going to be a profitable customer. There's really no difference between what an insurance company is trying to learn about their applicants and what lenders are trying to learn about theirs.

Second, all of the insurance companies that use your credit information to determine your insurance risk have performed studies called "validations" that prove time and time again that how you manage your credit has a direct correlation to the kind of insurance customer you will be. So, not only is it legal to use your credit information to determine insurance risk, but it's also a solid and statistically sound indicator.

Now that I've said all of that, I completely understand consumers' anger about this. How in the world does how I pay my bills influence whether or not I'm going to get run into from behind while I'm driving to work or whether or not a tree is going to fall through the roof of my home, thus forcing me to file insurance claims? The answer to those questions is…it doesn't. But, if you took 1,000 consumers with low credit scores and compared them with 1,000 consumers with high credit scores, the consumers with the high credit scores, as a group, are better insurance customers. Statistically, the high credit-scoring group files fewer claims. That's a fact, and that's how you have to think about this in order to not drive yourself crazy.

Are they the same scores?

The scores that the insurance companies use are different than the scores lenders use. "Insurance credit bureau scores" are built specifically to predict insurance-related outcomes, such as whether or not you're likely to file a claim or whether or not you're going to be a profitable insurance customer. Credit risk scores, on the other hand, are designed to predict the likelihood that you will (or will not) pay your lenders back on time.

Some insurance scores go beyond your credit information and evaluate your previous insurance claims information as well. If you've ever had to file a claim with your insurance company for a car wreck or some sort of home damages, that information can and probably will be used when calculating your insurance credit scores. As you can imagine, if you file claims frequently, you're more likely to file claims in the future, which makes you a less profitable insurance customer. That means your insurance scores will be lower and your premiums will likely be higher.

Who is ChoicePoint and why you should care about them?

Everyone knows who Equifax and TransUnion are. And, almost everyone remembers when TRW was in the credit reporting business. It got out of that business many years ago, and Experian bought its credit data and took its place among the "big three" ranks. You may not have ever heard of a company called ChoicePoint, however.

ChoicePoint used to be the Insurance Services division of Equifax. Many years ago, Equifax spun off their Insurance Services division into its own company, which named itself ChoicePoint. This company operated quietly under the radar for many years until it became headline news when identity thieves accessed its databases in early 2005 and more than 150,000 consumer records were compromised. It ended up paying several million dollars in fines.

The reason you should care about ChoicePoint is because it is to the insurance industry what Equifax, TransUnion, and Experian are to the credit industry. It is the premier provider of insurance reports and insurance scores to insurance companies. Whenever you apply for auto or homeowners insurance, your insurance company can and probably will pull your insurance claim report and score from ChoicePoint. The process is very similar to what happens when you apply for credit and your lenders pull your credit reports and scores. Is that news to you? Most people don't know that this happens in the insurance world and are quite surprised when they learn.

Do you have a CLUE®?

ChoicePoint gets its information (your claim information) from insurance companies. If you file an auto or homeowner's claim, the nature of the claim and the amount paid is reported to and stored by ChoicePoint. This information is sold to other insurance companies. The report that it sells is called a CLUE Report. CLUE stands for Comprehensive Loss Underwriting Exchange.

If you've filed an auto or home claim in the recent past, you have a CLUE report with ChoicePoint. If you've never filed any sort of insurance claim then you don't. The good news is that you can get a free copy of whatever they have in their system once a year just like you can with your credit reports. At the time of printing, the website where you could request your free CLUE report was www. choicetrust.com. Also, if you live in any of the states that allow for free credit reports, you are entitled to additional free CLUE reports. So, for example, a resident of Georgia can get 3 free copies of their CLUE reports each year, two because the individual lives in Georgia and one more because of federal law.

CLUE reports are a little different than credit reports. First, if you haven't filed an auto or homeowner claim in the past few years then you won't have a report. Second, ChoicePoint stores your auto and homeowner claims separately. That means you CAN have two separate CLUE reports, one each for auto and homeowner claims. So when you request your freebies, be sure to request both of them so you can see exactly what they are saying about you to insurance companies.

ChoicePoint's insurance credit score is the industry standard in the insurance world, much like the "FICO®" score built by Fair Isaac Corporation is the industry standard in the lending world. Its insurance score is called the "CP-Attract" score. Fair Isaac Corporation also builds insurance scores but doesn't get the benefit of ChoicePoint's insurance claim data, thus making it a less attractive option for insurance companies. You can get your CP-Attract scores at the ChoiceTrust website but there is a fee for it.

Chapter 10
Master's Level

The purpose of this chapter is to offer some more advanced credit-related information for the folks who are really interested in delving into this stuff. It's not everything, but if you master all of the following strategies then you'll certainly be ahead of the game..

What matters?

First and foremost, you must realize that how you manage your credit only matters to the extent that your credit reports reflect it. That means if you make all of your payments on time but none of your creditors report that information, you'll never get any credit for it in your credit scores. And, conversely, if you miss payments with a creditor that doesn't report to the credit bureaus then your scores will never suffer. Your credit reports and scores are only as accurate as the information that has been reported.

The credit reporting industry is largely a voluntary system. Lenders don't have to pull credit reports or scores and they certainly don't have to send your account and payment information to any company, the credit bureaus included. While most lenders do pull credit reports when you apply, you'd be surprised how many large national lenders don't report their accounts to all three credit bureaus. Try a little experiment: pull all three of your credit reports from the www. annualcreditreport.com site. That shouldn't cost you a dime. Then do an inventory of everything on your credit reports, including the number of accounts, the number of inquiries, the balances, late payments, and anything else you can find. You'll notice very quickly that the information isn't uniform across your three credit reports. That's a product of credit reporting being a voluntary system.

The byproduct of your actions

This section could also be called "collateral damage." A huge myth floating around in the credit score world is that all of your actions will have a specific point value. So, if you pay off a collection you'll get X points or if you apply for credit, that inquiry will lower your score by Y points. This is not true.

Anything you do with your credit will have an impact on several of the credit score categories that I talked about in Chapter 6. Let's take a look at what happens when you open a new credit card account. We'll call this the "anatomy of a credit card account."

John's Bank

Account #:	193xx-0939-xx	Date Reported:	02/07
Type:	Revolving	Current Balance:	$10,000
Pay Status:	Current	Credit Limit:	$25,000
Date Opened:	05/04	Previous Late Payments:	Pays As Agreed

Before this account was opened you had to apply for it, right? That means an inquiry from the credit card company will now show up on your credit report and it could lower your scores.

This credit card account will probably be reported to one or more of the credit reporting agencies. Since it has a very recent "opened" date, it will lower the average age of the accounts on your credit report. This can lower your scores.

The credit card account has a credit limit that has been assigned by the credit card issuer. Assuming it's being reported correctly on your credit reports, it could help your overall utilization and help your scores at the same time.

On the other hand, if this card carries a balance, it can lower your scores because you may now have more credit card debt than you did prior to opening that account. If the balance is too high it could hurt your utilization, thus lowering your scores.

The moral of this story is that your actions do not happen in a vacuum. By applying for this one credit card you will have impacted at least four out of the five credit score categories from Chapter 6. You'll help some and hurt others. The net effect of your actions won't be known until a new score is calculated taking into account all of the new data in your credit reports. So you see, you can't simply say, "Oh, I'll open a new account and it will help my score." It's not that easy.

Credit card utilization

By now this is probably review work, but I still think it's worth touching on again. Your credit card use is extremely important to your scores. In the uneducated credit user world this fact simply isn't that well known. The assumption is that as long as you are making your credit card payments, all is well. There is very little thought given to your balances and whether or not they are hurting your scores.

In fact, your balances, your credit limits, and your number of credit cards with a balance are all very important factors in your credit scores. So important that they are a very close second right behind whether or not you make your payments. So, making the minimum payments each month might be great for the "making your payments" category, but it's certainly not helping your debt-related category.

Here's how it works:

John's Bank

Account #:	193xx-0939-xx	Date Reported:	02/07
Type:	Revolving	Current Balance:	$5,000
Pay Status:	Current	Credit Limit:	$10,000
Date Opened:	05/04	Previous Late Payments:	Pays As Agreed

Dave's Bank

Account #:	456xx-3659-xx	Date Reported:	02/07
Type:	Revolving	Current Balance:	$5,000
Pay Status:	Current	Credit Limit:	$20,000
Date Opened:	07/06	Previous Late Payments:	Pays As Agreed

These are what credit card accounts typically look like on your credit report. From these examples we can conclude quite a few things about this consumer. First, we can conclude that he has two open credit card accounts. We can also conclude that he has two credit card accounts with balances. Pretty easy so far.

Here's where it gets a little more complex. We can also measure each individual account's utilization. That's the percentage of the credit limit you are currently utilizing. The first credit card is issued by John's Bank. The credit limit is $10,000 and the balance is $5,000. The John's Bank credit card is 50% utilized because the consumer is using up half of the credit limit. The second card issued by Dave's Bank has a credit limit of $20,000 and a balance of $5,000. The Dave's Bank credit card is 25% utilized because the consumer is using up 25% of the credit limit. Those percentages matter to your credit score.

Now you have to figure out the overall utilization percentage for all of the credit card accounts. In this case, we have to add up the credit limits and balances for all of the open credit card accounts. In the case mentioned earlier, the overall credit limit is $30,000 and the overall balance is $10,000. That would make this consumer 33% utilized because he is using up 33% of his total available credit limits. Again, that 33% says a lot about his credit risk and therefore it will have a huge impact on his credit scores.

For some reason people get the idea that as long as utilization is under 50% everything is fine. This misconception is both completely incorrect and very dangerous. If you really want to max out your credit scores, your utilization should be no higher than 10%. That poses a problem for some people because they depend so heavily on their credit cards that 10% isn't realistic. In the example above, that would mean the total credit card balances could never exceed $3,000. For consumers with much lower credit limits on their credit cards, card usage would be even more restricted.

The point here is that the 10% target is recommended only if you are trying to max out your scores. We're not always in the market for credit. In fact, we're rarely in the market for credit and the only time that we need to max out our scores is if we're about to apply for something. So, if you're not going to be applying for credit any time soon then it really doesn't matter what your balances are. But, if you are going credit shopping in the next 60 to 90 days, then you had better knock out those balances or at least get them to the 10% target if you want to get as high of a score as possible.

There are a couple of ways to tackle the problem of decreasing high utilization. You can lower your balances by paying them, of course. Or you can increase your credit limits. Or, you can do a little of both. This is nothing more than a division problem. If you can change the numbers that go into the equation, then you can and will change your utilization. But, be careful when you're asking your credit card issuers to increase your credit limits. They'll probably want to pull your credit report beforehand. We all know what that can do to your scores, so be careful.

Secured credit cards

What is a secured credit card? It's a credit card that is issued to you that is "secured" when you make a deposit with the issuing creditor. If you give the creditor $500, they'll give you a credit card with a $500 credit limit. If you don't make your payments then they'll just take it out of the deposit you made. Your deposit is their security, hence the name of the card.

Secured cards are not the best kinds of credit cards. In fact, some people would argue that they're the worst kind of credit cards. They have very high interest rates and fees. But, they aren't meant for everyone. They have a purpose. They're meant for people who are just starting out and are trying to establish credit or are trying to rebuild their credit after some sort of major credit-damaging life event, such as a divorce or a job loss.

When you are trying to rebuild, you need all of the good accounts on your credit reports that you can get. If you've got really bad credit, you will have to take what you can get until your credit reports and scores have improved to the point that you can get the good types of credit. Secured cards may be the only types of credit that you can get for a while.

The good news about secured cards is that when they show up on your credit reports, they don't adversely affect your scores. As long as they are being paid on time and your balances aren't excessive then they'll help your credit scores as much as any other high limit unsecured credit card would. And as long as your deposit check clears you'll probably get approved when you apply, subject to the lender's normal credit qualification standards, of course.

With a secured card you are basically buying the credit with your deposit. When your credit has been established or rebuilt and your scores are again impressive, you can either ask that the secured credit card issuer convert the account to an unsecured credit card or you can stop using it and perhaps even close it and get your deposit back (closing the account might not always be the best strategy for you, though, for reasons we talked about previously).

Authorized users - The lame duck strategy

What's an authorized user? An authorized user is someone who is added to a credit card account as someone who has the card and is allowed to use it but who isn't financially liable for any of the charges. They are simply "authorized" to use the card – that's all.

You may have been an authorized user on your parents' credit card accounts. Or you may have a child who is an authorized user on one of your credit card accounts. Here's a little secret that you may or may not know: Authorized user accounts are a great way to establish credit or rebuild your credit.

Some of the credit card issuers will actually report the account on the authorized user's credit reports. That means if the account is in good standing and the balance isn't too high, it will probably help the authorized user's credit scores. This is a very common way for children to establish credit. Their parents add them to their credit card accounts and the account shows up on the child's credit reports, creating a credit report with a good account and a good credit score.

This strategy is a very good one for the authorized user because they get the positive benefit of the account without any of the liability for the payments. And, if the parent or primary cardholder stops making payments or runs the balance too close to the credit limit, the authorized user can easily get the account removed by contacting the credit bureaus. Since they are not financially liable for the account it is easy to have it removed. In fact, at least one of the three credit bureaus has a policy where they won't even contact the credit card issuer as part of their verification process. They'll simply remove it when the consumer asks that it be removed.

Chapter 10: Master's Level

The only problem with this strategy is that it will eventually cease to work. Fair Isaac has made the decision to exclude authorized user accounts from its scoring models. By the end of 2008 this strategy will no longer work.

Since the additional card will be mailed to the primary cardholder, it's possible that the authorized user never even gets a card. That way the primary won't have to worry about the authorized user making purchases with the card. It's a win-win for both parties.

Minimizing the impact of credit inquiries

We know that inquires can lower your credit scores. And, we also know that you have to be able to apply for credit when you need it, right? You may want to buy a house, you probably already bought a car, and you probably have credit cards and will apply for more credit in the next few months or years. You shouldn't be afraid to apply for credit just because of the impact that the inquiry will have on your scores. They're a necessarily evil and there's nothing you can do to avoid them.

There is, however, something you can do to minimize the impact of the inquiries to your credit scores. It's something I call "strategic shopping." You can do this by taking advantage of a little-known secret built within the most commonly used credit scoring models, the FICO® score.

Many years ago, the developers at Fair Isaac, creators of the FICO scoring models, modified their models to treat inquiries in such a way that doesn't penalize a consumer who is shopping for a good interest rate on a car or a home loan, as long as they do all of their rate shopping in a fairly short amount of time.

Here's how it works: credit inquiries are coded so that it's very easy to tell who the lender was who pulled your credit report and in what industry they lend. So, for example, a "John's Used Cars" inquiry would be easily identified as a used car inquiry. It is this coding that allows the FICO scores to do their magic.

Any auto or mortgage-related inquiries don't count against your scores – at all – for the first 30 days that they exist. That means you can shop all you want for a great auto or home loan rate and not have to worry about the inquiries for 30 days. You should be able to get your rate shopping done within 30 days.

If you cannot get your rate shopping done in 30 days then there's even a backup plan programmed into the scores. After those inquiries become older than 30 days, any of them that occur within 14 days of each other will only count as one inquiry in the scoring model. In some of the newer FICO score versions, the 14-day period has been expanded to 45 days. So, for example, if I shopped around at 20 different car dealerships for the best deal and all of them pulled my credit reports and scores, in theory that would mean I should now have 20 auto dealer inquiries on my credit report.

All of those 20 inquiries are coded "auto finance," which means that for 30 days they don't count at all. They are "bypassed." Then, after 30 days, any of them that occur within 14 days of each other only count as one inquiry.

As you can see, this system is very consumer-friendly. The goal of the credit-scoring model is to determine how many loans you are applying for. In this case, you are only looking for one auto loan, so your score should only be penalized the equivalent of one inquiry. That's the purpose of this little-known score secret.

Not that this factored into the decision to come up with this consumer-friendly inquiry treatment, but penalizing consumers' scores every time they apply for credit doesn't make very good business sense. Every time the credit bureaus sell your credit reports to lenders they make money. And, it's in their best financial interest to sell a lot of credit reports. Fair Isaac also makes money every time one of their scores is sold to lenders by one of the credit bureaus. So this inquiry logic not only treats consumers better but it's also a wise business decision on behalf of Fair Isaac.

Be careful who you listen to

So much incorrect information about credit reports and credit scores is floating around. The press is to blame for this; so are mortgage lenders, car dealers, and any other so-called "experts" who are advising consumers on how to better their credit ratings. The reality is that unless you are or have been intimately involved with credit reports and credit scoring models, you shouldn't be giving anyone advice about how to better manage credit.

I estimate that about 75% of what I read in the press about credit scores is correct. That means 25% is incorrect.

Improving credit scores is very much like performing surgery on someone. It's very complex. What might seem right could actually cause significant damage. Any advice that you listen to should come from a true expert, just like any medical advice you take should come from a doctor. Here are some of the more common myths and INCORRECT advice that can lead consumers down the wrong path:

- ➥ Close your credit card accounts if you are not using them.

- ➥ When an account has been paid off, it is a good idea to try and get it removed from your credit reports.

- ➥ Live debt free; it will improve your scores.

- ➥ Settling a debt (such as a tax lien) will improve your scores.

•❖ Paying off collections will remove them from your credit reports.

•❖ Keeping your credit card balances at or near 50% of your credit limits will improve your credit scores.

•❖ Your age, race, level of education, where you live, income, and net worth count in your scores.

•❖ Home Equity accounts will always lower your credit scores because credit-scoring models interpret them as credit cards.

•❖ Inquiries are worth 5 points each (or any other exact point value).

•❖ A Chapter 13 bankruptcy is better for your credit scores than a Chapter 7 bankruptcy.

Every single one of the above statements is flat-out INCORRECT. And, if it's given to you as advice and you follow it, beware! You just might hurt your scores.

Buyer beware when it comes to scores that are for sale to the public

Some companies sell non-FICO credit scores directly to consumers and in many cases they are not the same scores that are sold to lenders. Because of the potential downside to consumers resulting from this practice, I'm going to focus the remainder of this chapter on providing as much detail as I can about these companies and their scores. Armed with this information, you'll be able to make a more informed decision about whether or not to buy their credit score products.

The downside for consumers when it comes to offering them multiple score product options is that they often come with advice on how to improve them. You have to be very careful when taking "score improvement" advice from a company who is marketing a non-FICO score. As you've no doubt learned from reading this book, your credit actions can and almost always will have an impact on your FICO credit scores, the ones that lender and insurance companies see and use. It is very possible that you might do something to improve one "brand" of credit score, and at the same time you may lower your FICO scores.

Here are the companies that sell non-FICO credit scores

Experian – That's right: One of the big three credit reporting agencies. It sells your FICO credit score (developed by the Fair Isaac Corporation) to lenders but also markets and sells to consumers a score that's different. Its "consumer" score is called the PLUS Score™. Experian sells it at a number of different web sites, all marketed under different brands. Be very careful when watching commercials about free credit reports; that's one of the marketing tactics. You're not buying your FICO score from Experian.

TransUnion – Again, one of the big three credit reporting agencies. It sells your real FICO credit score to lenders, but then they sell you a score that's different. TransUnion's is called the TransRisk score, which actually is also available for sale to lenders…but just isn't commonly used. TransUnion markets these scores under their "TrueCredit" brand. If you are a tenacious surfer you might find the small off-colored text that says that it is not selling a FICO score. TransUnion does sell the legitimate FICO credit score to consumers, but it's marketed at their TransUnion Consumer Services website which is next to impossible to find. Check it out at www.transunioncs. com.

Intersections – This company markets credit monitoring services directly to consumers and through its partnerships with other companies. You probably have seen its products, but branded under your bank's name. That's called "private labeling." They sell credit reports and non-FICO scores as well. Their score is called the CreditXpert score, built by a company called Neuristics, Inc. And, yes again, no lenders use it. Intersetions even disclaims its own score by saying in its user agreement that its score is not a FICO score. Why does it even bother? What is it trying to hide?

PrivacyGuard – As with Intersections, this company markets credit-monitoring services directly to consumers and through its partnerships with other companies. You certainly have seen their products branded under another name. Its sells credit reports and non-FICO scores as well. It also uses the CreditXpert score.

Another problem with these non-FICO scores is the score range that they choose to use for their scores. The score range of the industry standard FICO score is 300 to 850. All of the above companies use a score range that is very similar to 300 to 850. Many consumers become confused when they see a score range so similar to the FICO score, especially when it is not clearly spelled out that it is not a FICO score.

As a former credit score model developer I can tell you that any credit-scoring model can be built with any range. They can be 0 to 100, A-Z, 1000 to 2000; anything they want. But, these companies consciously chose a score range that is so very similar to the FICO score range. Why do you think that's so?

Does anything here strike you as odd?

- *PLUS Score* – 330-830 (according to their website)
- *TransRisk Score* – 300-850 (according to a chart on the TrueCredit site)
- *Intersections/CreditXpert* – 350-850 (according to my own account with them)
- *PrivacyGuard* – 350-850 (according to their website)

⇄ *FICO Scores* – 300-850

Is it luck, or have all of these companies purposely built their non-FICO credit scores to perhaps make people believe that they're buying the real thing? Buyer beware!

Chapter 11
Kids and Credit

I can still remember when I used to sit down next to my father while he was writing the checks to pay our monthly bills. He would explain exactly what each check was for, show me how to write it, seal it, stamp it, and mail it. One of the most memorable comments he made each month was the following: "John, if you can make your payments every single month without ever missing one, you'll be all right."

Of course, at my age I didn't really understand what he was talking about. What did he mean by "all right?" Now that I'm older and wiser, I realize exactly the point he was making. The point was that if I made all of my payments on time then I would have great credit. And with great credit I could borrow money from banks or other lenders without any trouble. At that time in our nation's credit "history," that was exactly right. As long as you made your payments on time, all was well.

That was long before credit scoring became the lending and insurance industry's standard method to determine consumer credit and insurance risk. What my father taught me was 100% correct. As long as I paid my bills on time I was considered a safe credit risk. I could get credit from anyone, anywhere, any time.

Fast forward to today, where there is very little human interaction when a credit application is processed. Once your application is submitted, a credit report is pulled, your scores are calculated, and a pre-determined decision is made. All this happens in a few seconds and involves nothing but machines. Some people would argue that we've gained efficiency and removed human bias. Others would argue that we've removed common sense and years of experience from the lending process.

That's the new reality in the credit and insurance world. It's something that new credit users and younger generations will become more and more used to. It's something that the older generations don't really understand and don't really like.

So, rather than telling your children to simply pay their bills on time, I'm going to suggest that you tell them a much longer story. One that includes a statement that paying your bills on time is very important, but there's more to it than that. It's only one part of the number lenders are relying more and more on: your credit scores. Here is my advice:

For younger kids

Once your children reach the age where they start getting an allowance, it's probably a good time to start mixing in a little credit training. When they start getting the allowance, they'll start to appreciate the value of money and what it can buy for them, but it won't teach them the value of sound credit management. Most parents give their children an allowance in exchange for them performing some sort of task, such as chores around the house. Perhaps a slightly modified version of this can be used to teach your children about credit.

Instead of simply giving your children money after they've performed some sort of task, I suggest giving them several weeks' worth of allowance all up front. Explain to your child that you are giving them this allowance "on credit" and you expect them to perform their normal tasks over the next several weeks as they normally do. This method of advancing them the money will be much easier for them to understand than it will be for you to try and explain payment schedules and interest rates. All they need to know is that they've been given a couple of months' worth of their allowance all at one time before they actually perform their household chores. They've been given a loan and the expected payback is for them to continue performing their chores as they have agreed.

What will probably happen is your child will spend all of the money very quickly and then ask for more. For the purposes of this exercise, that's fine. Give them another few weeks' worth of allowance and explain to them that they've just taken out another "advance" and that now they owe you even more weeks… but now there's a catch. Since you are advancing them money, you want them to perform an extra hour worth of work per week for the next month. That will be your equivalent of interest on your loan.

Play around with this so it works for your family. If money isn't something you want to introduce to your children yet then use something else that they value. We use television time as our currency whenever our nieces visit us. Our deal is this: you can watch an hour of television, but only if you eat a full helping of green beans. If you want to have two hours of television, you have to try something new. The last time they visited they tried sushi, which was very traumatic. But, they tried it and we rewarded them with two hours of television. We got something from them, and they got something from us.

Once we got them hooked on the television time, something their mother probably doesn't appreciate too much, we started to play the credit game with them. Now, we offer them television time on the promise that they will eat their veggies the following day. I've never failed to make a deal with my nieces that as long as they will commit to eating some new food or vegetable that they can have their television time right now.

Of course, when I remind them the following day that they owe me a helping of broccoli, they try to talk me out of it. But a deal is a deal. And since I can't repossess the time they spent in front of the television from the night before, I want something from them. That something is my credit payment. In this case, we'll get some help with the laundry or maybe even get them to wash dishes. It's amazing that at the ages of 6 and 12 they've already mastered a skill that millions of adults are having trouble with. Now they actually think about the TV deals before they make them, as if they are thinking about the consequences of taking on credit.

Have fun with this. Be as lenient or as strict as you want to be. Incorporate a reward such as money, video games, toys, TV or computer time, or something else that your kids love as much as we love money. By the time your children head off into the real world, they'll have a solid understanding of credit and the consequences of abusing it.

As a country, we are grossly undereducated about credit. When I was in high school, you could actually take Home Economics classes and learn how to stuff pillows, sew a button, and use an iron. You could take Shop and Vocational classes and learn to use a table saw and retread tires. And you could learn Geometry, Calculus, and Biology. But, there isn't a single class offered in any school at any level that teaches children how to establish and properly manage their credit. It's a shame, because most of us will use credit from the time we are in our late teens or early twenties, and we'll use it for the rest of our life!

That's usually at least a half of a century that we'll spend in what I call the "consumer credit lifecycle." How do we learn about this process? We learn it through trial and error. And, since there are very few legitimate resources that can teach this stuff, some people never really learn to use credit the right way.

For teenagers

At some point, the value of television time will go away and will be replaced by the all-mighty dollar. For most of us, this happens during our teenage years. We start driving, which means we may have to pay for gas or insurance, and we're almost certainly driving to places like the mall, restaurants, and even going on dates. All of this requires money, so our focus shifts sharply from the non-monetary currency over to the dollar.

This shift marks the perfect time to start helping your children establish their credit reports. Remember: they only get one chance to do this, so the more you can help them do it right, the better off they'll be for years to come. There are a couple ways to help your children establish credit. You can add them to your existing credit card accounts, you can co-sign on a loan for them, and you can even let them open up an account in their name only and make their payments for them. Each of these scenarios has pros and cons. None of them are perfect, and none of them are terrible. Here are the details:

Adding them to your existing credit card accounts

This is probably the most common way parents help their children establish credit. You can add them to your existing credit card accounts as "authorized users," which means that they have a card with their name on it and they can make purchases. They just aren't financially liable for the payments. That's still your responsibility.

Some credit card issuers will add the account to your authorized user's credit reports. This will create a credit file for them if they don't already have one. The account that's on their credit files is YOUR account. It will look exactly like the account that shows up on your credit files except it will clearly note that your child is an authorized user on the account.

The good news is that if your account is in good standing, has always been paid on time, and the balance isn't excessive, your children will benefit because of the good account. It will not only help them build their credit files but it will also help them build their credit scores. And, you can choose to not actually give them the credit card with their name imprinted on it. That will serve as an insurance policy against them possibly abusing the card.

The best news with this strategy is that since your children are not liable for the account, they can easily have it removed from their credit reports. If the account ever becomes delinquent or the balance gets out of control, they can simply have it removed. There is very little, if any, risk to either party.

As mentioned in the previous chapter, this strategy won't work after 2008. But, you can still add your child as an authorized user to your credit card accounts and teach them how to use and manage credit cards responsibly. They just won't get any credit in their credit files and scores any longer.

Co-signing

Co-signing is another way to help establish credit for your children. Basically, you are agreeing to be financially liable for an account that your child opens. You sign the contract along with your child, which makes you a "co-signer."

Much like the authorized user strategy above, co-signing will likely result in an account being reported to your credit files and your child's credit files. If the account remains in good standing and the balance stays at a reasonable level, the account will help your child's credit file as well as yours. The only difference is the account that shows up on your child's credit files with you as a clear co-signer. Other than that, there's no difference in the appearance of the account.

The danger with co-signed accounts is that both parties are financially liable. That means if your child cannot or will not make the payments according to the terms of the loan contract, either you have to make them or both of your credit reports will be damaged by late payments. And, unlike an authorized user account, you won't be able to get the co-signed account removed from either of your credit files because you are both liable for the debt.

Be very careful when co-signing for loans. You'll have to be prepared to take over the payments or your credit could be damaged. It will certainly help build your child's credit files, but you're also counting on his or her ability to properly manage the debt.

Opening their own accounts, with your help

Another option is to maintain an arm's length between your credit and your children's credit but still offer a safety net in case anything happens. Let them open an account on their own. Suggest a gasoline credit card or a retail store card. The credit limits on these accounts are normally very low and they're usually very easy to get approved.

Since the credit limits are so low, it will prevent your children from getting too deep into debt. But, it will also penalize their scores because even a small amount of usage will result in a very high utilization percentage. This will be like training wheels for them. If they max out their card, they'll feel the sting of a lower score, but that can easily be fixed by paying off the balance in full the following month.

Over time, the credit card accounts will get older and older, which will help their scores. As their scores get higher and higher, the credit card issuers will likely give them credit line increases. That too will help their scores. Eventually, when you're ready to cut them loose to manage the accounts on their own, they'll have excellent scores because of decent "aging" and low utilization. You will have done your job.

The EKG effect

You know what an EKG is, yes? It's an Electrocardiogram. This is a test that measures the activity of a heartbeat. If you've never seen an EKG, it looks like this.

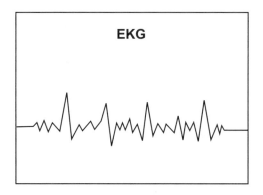

That EKG graph looks very similar to what can happen to a young person's credit scores. You see, your scores change as things on your credit reports change. One day your scores can be 700, 710, and 715 and the next day they can be 720, 740 and 745. This is called "score movement" and it happens to every single one of us. But, score movement for a young person can be a problem.

The older and longer your credit reports become, the more stable your scores will be. That's because someone who has 20 years and 10 pages worth of credit history isn't going to see their scores change all that much by opening a new account or making a major purchase on a credit card. In the grand scheme of things, their actions didn't really change their credit all that much. As such, their credit scores will remain pretty much the same.

For a young person who only has one or two accounts that have only been opened for a few years, adding a new account or charging a large amount to a credit card is a very significant change to their credit file. And, this large change will result in a very large score change. This can be a huge problem, especially if your child is trying to get a student loan, a car loan, a job, or anything else that depends upon your credit files or credit scores. One day their credit reports look great and the next day they look not so great.

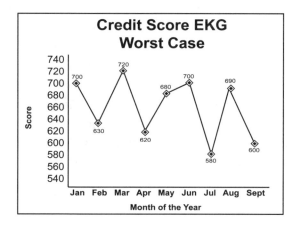

This is not how you want your scores to fluctuate over time. But, this is typical of a young person's score movement. Even the smallest changes to credit reports may drastically impact scores. In this example above, the consumer's score changes wildly month after month. It's hard for this person to know what kind of response he or she will get upon applying for credit because the score goes from as low as 580 all the way up to 720, depending on how he or she managed credit the previous month.

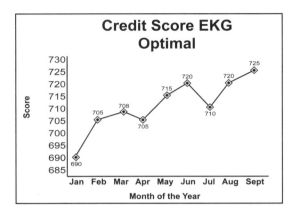

Now this is more like it. You'll notice that this person's score stays within 35 points for the entire amount of time measured. This is good because the consumer always knows roughly where his or her score will be and can shop for credit accordingly. This person knows that he or she will get approved with a very competitive offer and can focus on lenders who do business with low-risk consumers.

Chapter 12

How Do Lenders
Use Your Credit Reports and Scores?

T he purpose of this chapter is to give you an insider's peak into how different companies use your credit reports and credit scores. And, we'll also address some of the more secretive ways your personal information is used that aren't generally known.

What you need to understand is that there are multiple industries that use your credit reports and scores, and they don't necessarily all use them the same way. In fact, they all use them pretty differently in an effort to determine the same thing...your credit risk. We'll go through each industry one at a time and I'll explain exactly how they do this.

Auto lending

In the auto world, lenders use your credit reports and scores as a way to determine whether or not you deserve to be approved for an auto loan or lease and according to what terms. But, unlike any other industry, auto lenders have a very large number of "offers" that they can make to a consumer based upon their credit scores. That means each of these lenders has to create and maintain what's referred to in the industry as a "tiered pricing schedule." In laymen's terms, this means a chart that tells them what they can offer you based upon your credit score. Here is an example of one of these charts.

John's Auto Lot
Pricing Schedule

Score	Interest Rate	Down Payment Requirements
less than 600	21%	20%
600-624	13%	15%
625-649	11.5%	10%
650-674	10.5%	10%
675-699	8%	5%
700 or above	6.5%	none

For example, if your score falls into the 625-649 range then the dealer will offer you an interest rate of 11.5% and will require that you put down 10%.

As mentioned earlier, since there are three credit reporting agencies, you have three credit reports and three credit scores. Auto lenders can choose which ones they want to use when you apply for a car loan. You have no input in that decision, so you have to live with whatever information they are given from whatever credit bureau they use.

While your credit reports and therefore your credit scores should be fairly similar, there are many cases where they can vary wildly. This can cause problems when you apply for an auto loan because the lender may be pulling your credit report from the credit bureau where your credit score is the lowest, or where it's simply not the highest. This isn't good for you.

The reason auto lenders generally only pull one report is because credit reports and scores aren't free. It's an investment for the lender to buy your credit reports and scores when you apply. And while it's only a few dollars at most, that can add up. In an effort to protect their margins, auto lenders will generally decide to pull one of your three credit reports. That doesn't mean they don't have the ability to pull two or even all three of your reports. Almost all car dealerships and lenders have accounts with all three credit bureaus, which provides them with the ability to pull as many of your reports as they want. If they can't find your report from their primary provider, they'll defer to their secondary and then tertiary provider until they get your information

Mortgage lending

In the mortgage world, the credit and lending process is unique and confusing. When you apply for a mortgage loan, the lender (or broker) will almost always buy all three of your credit reports and scores. If you apply with someone else, like your spouse, they'll buy all three of your spouse's reports as well. That means they'll be making their decision with three to six credit reports and three to six credit scores.

They have everything they need to evaluate your credit risk. You can't hide anything from your mortgage lender. If you have anything negative on any of your credit reports, your mortgage lender will know about it.

It is very standard in the mortgage industry for the lender to use the middle of your three scores. So, if your scores are 700, 710, and 720, the lender will use your 710 to determine your credit risk and therefore the loan offer that they will make to you. It doesn't matter which of the three credit bureaus was the one that generated the 710; the score is what's important.

To add yet another wrinkle to this particular credit-reporting puzzle, I'll introduce you to a new term: a credit report reseller. There is an entire industry of companies that resell credit information that the three national credit reporting agencies house. These resellers have become a mainstay in the mortgage world because of their ability to consolidate the information from the three credit bureaus into one easier to read report that the mortgage lender can use.

Remember: Mortgage lenders get at least three credit reports and more often six. That's a lot of information, and *duplicate* information in fact. It's confusing and time-consuming to read and understand. The service that these reseller companies offer is a merging of all of your (and your co-applicant's) credit information. They deliver an easy-to-read, consolidated credit report.

These companies do not change your information, they do not calculate your scores, and they certainly didn't report any of the information originally. If you have ever applied for a mortgage, you probably got a copy of your merged credit reports at closing. In fact, that's now a law under the newest amendment to the Fair Credit Reporting Act. Mortgage lenders are required to give you a copy of your credit information at closing. You don't even need to ask for it.

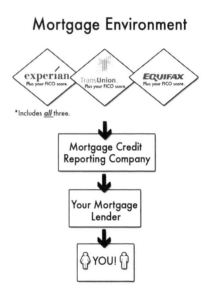

Mortgage Environment

Credit card issuers

This includes anything that's plastic in your wallet other than your debit or check cards. Gasoline credit cards and retail store cards are included in this category as well as the standard Visa, Discover, American Express and MasterCard products.

The credit card world is fairly similar to the auto world in that your scores are used to determine credit risk and are used to set your interest rate. Since a credit card has a credit limit (the maximum amount that you can charge on the card), your scores are used to set that amount as well. But that's where the similarity ends.

Non-Mortgage Environment

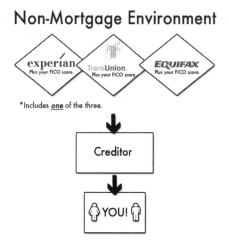

*Includes *one* of the three.

Creditor

YOU!

The primary difference between an auto loan and a credit card is that an auto loan has a fixed number of payments over a fixed number of months. This is called an installment loan. And since the payments are going to be same for the entire limited life of the loan, the auto lender really only has one chance to "set" the interest rate and other terms of the loan.

With a credit card, the payment is different each month and the account can be open as long as both the creditor and the consumer chose to keep it open. The payment is different because the balance is normally different each month. This is called a revolving account.

Account management and account review

With credit card accounts, the creditors are in it for the long haul rather than just for four or five years like with an auto loan. As such, they are very interested in always knowing what kind of credit risk you pose to them over time. The only way for them to always know what kind of risk you pose is to review how you manage your account with them…and with your other creditors.

These processes are called "account management" and "account review." What happens during both of these is the creditor will review all of the details of your existing account with them and with your other creditors. They do this very frequently, monthly in many cases. They always want to know how you are managing your accounts.

Part of the process is reviewing the information on your credit reports. This includes getting your credit scores. If they see that all is well with your other accounts, you'll probably never hear from them. However, if they see that you are having trouble with other accounts, like running up very high balances or missing payments, they have every right to change the terms of the credit card account.

In many cases, the creditor will decrease your credit limit so that you can't take on any more debt on their card. And, they will also likely increase your interest rate significantly so that your payments go up. This is all completely legal, even though it may seem to be very unfair.

Prescreening

Have you ever wondered why you get all of those credit card offers in the mail? I realize that you probably get offers for other types of credit, but by far the most mail you get from lenders is from the credit card guys. There's a reason you get their offers. And, there's a reason you get the types of offers that you get from them. This isn't random. In fact, it's quite a scientific process.

Almost all credit card issuers acquire new customers, among other ways, by pre-qualifying large lists of consumers and mailing them invitations to become customers. These lists often come from the credit reporting agencies, which sell your information to any lender who has a product they'd like to offer you.

Remember that credit reporting agencies all have somewhere in the neighborhood of 250 million consumers in their databases. That's a pretty big list. And while the credit card issuers would love to send their offers to everyone in the credit bureau's databases, they know they can't do that. They can't do it because not everyone is a good fit for their products. This is where the process called "prescreening" begins.

Prescreening is exactly what it sounds like. The credit card issuers want to screen your credit before they send you any offer. If you are a good fit for them, they'll send you an offer; if you are not, they won't. It's pretty simple. But how do they do this? What is the process? How can you get out of being on the credit bureau's lists that they sell to lenders? There are good answers to all of these questions.

Let's walk through an example of how we, if we were credit card issuers, might select a list of consumers to whom we want to mail an offer. First off, we have to think of a product that we want to entice them with. In this case, we'll come up with a really great product called the John's Bank Diamond Card. This credit card comes with a $50,000 credit limit and a 5% interest rate. It's a very good credit card. But, I don't want people to have it unless they are going to be very low credit risks. And I only want to offer that card to people who live in the Atlanta area.

I call up my credit bureau sales representative and I tell him, "I want to buy a list of everyone who lives in the metropolitan Atlanta area who has a credit score of at least 780." He takes my criteria and uses it to filter through everyone in the database who lives in Atlanta. Once he's done, he has a nice meaty list of probably several hundred thousand people who have met my minimum criteria.

Then he'll send those names to me or another company who I've hired to send out my offers. Most banks don't have an in-house mail center and use outside firms for this. They're the ones who send out all of the credit card offers. Within about thirty days, people start getting mail from John's Bank telling them that they have been pre-approved for our Diamond Card. Now you have a general idea why you get so many offers from credit card issuers.

Since your credit scores are used to qualify you for certain products, it's actually pretty easy to get an idea as to what your scores are like without actually having to buy them somewhere. All you have to do is read the offers you're receiving. If you are getting offers of the "gold" or "platinum" variety with very high credit limits, you can bet that your scores are pretty good. If you are getting offers with low credit limits from finance companies then you're scores are not very good.

Both account management and prescreening require that the credit bureaus access information from your credit reports. This will require that they post an inquiry in the name of the lender who performed the account management or prescreening. The good news is that the type of inquiry that is posted is the type of inquiry that will not hurt your credit scores. And, in fact, the only person who will ever see these inquiries is you. Lenders don't ever see them if they are there because of account management and prescreening processes.

Now, if you respond to one of their offers by signing the application and sending it in, you are giving them permission to pull your credit report and score for the purposes of opening your account and setting the terms of the credit card. When they do so, an inquiry will post that can lower your scores. Read the fine print on the offer when in comes in the mail and always remember: "The big print giveth and the fine print taketh away." When you send the application back to them you are applying for credit and giving them permission to pull your credit reports and scores.

If you do not want your name to ever be sold to lenders by the credit bureaus, you can have your data excluded. This is called "opting out." You can opt-out for free by going to the official Opt out website which is www.optoutprescreen.com. You can also opt out by calling 1-888-567-8688. This information is also included in any prescreened credit offer you get in the mail. It's a requirement. The font size might be tiny and hard to read, but it's there.

I've been opted-out for years, and I still receive some credit offers in the mail. Remember that by opting out you are just prohibiting the credit bureaus from selling your name to lenders. There isn't any way you can prevent other companies from selling your contact information. So while opting out definitely reduces the amount of junk mail you'll get, it won't eliminate it completely. I highly suggest that you opt-out.

Chapter 13

The Three C's:
Capacity, Collateral, and Creditworthiness

In my introduction, I made a bold comment that your income, debt-to-income ratio, and net worth are irrelevant when it comes to your credit scores, as are your assets and holdings. This dispels a very prevalent myth in the credit world that your "value" has some bearing on your credit scores and makes lenders treat you better than someone without the same level of wealth. It's very hard to believe even after being told time and time again that your income doesn't matter.

I still have a hard time accepting it, despite knowing that it's true and despite being able to prove it. Think about the last time you applied for a credit card or a car loan. Did you show them anything to prove that you were employed? Or proof of income? You may have been asked to fill that in as part of your application, but you didn't have to prove it. If they cared so much about your income, you would have been asked to produce your last few paycheck stubs.

In the credit and insurance worlds, there are several measurements that determine whether or not you're going to be approved for a loan, insurance, or some other benefit. While all of these measurements are designed to evaluate different things, the question they really want answered is whether you will be a profitable or a risky customer. If you are not going to be profitable (or don't have the potential to be), you're going to be declined or approved with terms so unattractive that they will essentially force you to be profitable.

These measurements are commonly referred to as "the three Cs." They stand for Capacity, Collateral, and Creditworthiness.

Capacity

In the credit world, capacity is your ability to make your payments. This is where all of the income-related measurements come into play. If you have a loan that requires you to make a payment of $1000 each month, then do you have enough of an income or assets to make the payment? That's capacity.

Capacity is very important to some lenders and secondary to others. In my example above with the credit card and auto loan applications, capacity was secondary. However, for some lenders, like mortgage lenders, your capacity is just as important as anything else.

When you apply for a mortgage, the mortgage lender or mortgage broker will likely pull all three of your credit reports and all three of your credit scores. If you apply jointly with someone else, they will pull all three of the second person's reports and scores as well. That's six credit reports and six credit scores. In addition to all of the credit reports, you will be required to prove your income by providing copies of recent paycheck stubs or even tax documents. This is their way of determining if you'll be able to make your monthly mortgage payments. It's their way of measuring your capacity.

There are some really great stories about maids and other domestic service people actually getting approved for loans at better terms then their very wealthy employers. The one that sticks out in my mind is a friend from Birmingham, Alabama. Barry is a private chef for a very wealthy surgeon. A few years ago, when the automakers were offering 0% financing, Barry went out and purchased a new SUV on credit. His credit was good enough to get him the 0% deal. When Barry's employer noticed his new SUV, he asked if he got a good deal. When Barry told him that he got it at 0%, the wealthy doctor figured it was time for a new car, so he went to the same dealership and applied for a loan.

First off, the doctor is so wealthy that he could have paid cash for the new car without blinking an eye. But his attitude was that if it was free money, why would he pay cash for it? It's actually a smart move on his part. He can earn interest on his money while it sits in the bank but he can't earn a dime on it if he gives it all to the car dealer in a lump sum. So, at 0% interest, it made smart financial sense to pay for it over four years.

The problem is that his credit wasn't the best in the world. In fact, it wasn't good at all. Not only did he not get the 0% offer, which was reserved for the credit elite, but he didn't even get approved with a single-digit interest rate. His offer was 14.9%, which is horrible. After the initial shock wore off, he argued with the salesman that he made so much money that his credit had to be good. Sorry Doc, it doesn't work that way.

Collateral

Collateral is the measurement that focuses on the value of the asset you are trying to buy on credit. So, for example, if I am trying to buy a car that is worth $25,000, the collateral of the loan that I take out is the value of the car. The same holds true for buying a house. If you buy a house that costs $500,000, that amount is the collateral of the loan you open to pay for it.

Collateral is only used in the installment loan world. An installment loan is a loan that has a fixed payment for a fixed number of months, such as a mortgage. The lender is going to want to be sure that the amount of money they lend you makes sense as compared to the value of the item that you are buying. For example, if you want to borrow $500,000 to buy a house, the lender is going to want to know if the house is worth at least $500,000.

The reason that's important is if the lender ever has to foreclose your home (or repossess your car), they want to be sure that they'll be able to recover their money by selling the asset. If they let you borrow $500,000 on a home, they'll want to know it's worth at least that amount. They'll figure that out by having an appraisal done on the home before they'll approve your loan application.

It's very unlikely that a lender would ever let you borrow much more than the appraised value of a home or a car. Those lenders don't stay in business long. There were lenders years ago that would do "125% LTV" loans. That meant they would let you borrow 125% of the appraised value of a home. Many of those lenders went out of business because of the losses they sustained. It's hard to find that type of loan today and if you do, your credit better be excellent.

Creditworthiness

This is the brass ring. Everyone is concerned about creditworthiness. That's no surprise. We're all aware of credit reports and we're all aware that there are credit scores. What we don't completely understand is that the term "creditworthy" means more than just "good credit" versus "bad credit."

Imagine if lenders and insurance companies only did business with good credit and insurance risks. That would certainly leave a lot of people uninsured and not "bankable." Bankable means that banks are willing to do business with you because they've determined you are someone who will be a profitable customer. If lenders and insurance companies only extended offers to those with great credit, they wouldn't be making any money off of higher risk consumers, which of course they love to do.

"Creditworthy" simply means a bank or insurance company has determined that they will approve you because they think they can make money off of you. It's doesn't really mean that you have good credit. It simply means that your credit is good enough.

That brings me to another myth about credit scoring, the one that says anyone with a score of 700 or greater is considered a good credit risk. That's a big mistake, and people who think it's true often settle for credit and insurance offers that aren't the best available.

The truth is that a score of 700 will get you a cup of coffee and about 125,000,000th in line. That's right, a 700 is right about the midpoint of where everyone scores in this country. If you believe that the credit bureaus are housing roughly 250,000,000 credit files, a 700 gets you about half way to the top scoring percentiles.

If this is confusing to you, perhaps this illustration will help:

National Distribution of Credit Scores

If your score is:

500 **you're in the lowest scoring 1%**
(this means that 99% of the people in this country score higher than you)

600 **you're in the lowest scoring 18%**

700 **you're in the lowest scoring 43%** ➤ *No, we're not kidding!*
(believe it or not, this is below average)

800 **you're in the highest scoring 10%**
(this means that you score higher than 90% of the people in this country)

Just because you're not scoring in the top percentiles doesn't mean that you are "bad." Lenders will generally consider anyone above 750 as being worthy of their best offers, despite the fact that it's a good 100 points off of the highest score possible. What this means is that most people in this country have good credit and good credit scores. That's why a 700 only gets you to about the 50th percentile nationally.

Chapter 14

Why All Credit Reports Are Inaccurate

Hopefully by now you realize just how helpless and dependent we are on the credit reporting and credit scoring industry. And, you should also realize that they control so much of what we are able to do when it comes to obtaining and using credit and insurance. These industries even control our ability to get and maintain employment. Since credit is so important in our lives, for so long, you'd probably think the entire system is highly advanced and continuously improving itself for the sake of us consumers. You'll be surprised and probably angry to find out that's simply not the case. The purpose of this chapter is to give you some real insight into what I believe to be a huge problem plaguing the credit reporting industry.

> *"They're all wrong, 100% of them."*

I'll go so far as to call the credit reporting industry a dinosaur that hasn't done nearly enough to stay with the times or take advantage of today's technological capabilities. Let's just put it this way: If you had taken a guided tour of the credit bureaus' database facilities 20 years ago, you'd hear many of the same things in a tour today.

For this chapter, I have to separate credit reports and credit scores. Credit scores are not what I'm talking about in this chapter. Credit scoring models have become more advanced over the past two decades thanks to continued research and development by the companies that build the models. I'm specifically referring to the credit reporting agencies – those huge warehouses that collect, maintain, and then sell your information to anyone who has a legal right to buy it.

There are three specific issues I believe support my argument that all credit reports contain big inaccuracies. And I'm not talking about a misspelling of a name or an old employer being reported as your current employer. I'm referring specifically to high value information that is important enough that it can make or break a loan, insurance application, or even a job. Here are the issues:

A voluntary system

The system of credit reporting is largely voluntary. That means your lenders have a choice as to what, if, how often, and to whom they report your account information. On the surface, this might seem like a good thing, but when you start peeling back the onion you quickly find out that it's a huge disservice to consumers to have a system that's based upon voluntary credit reporting.

In order to clearly illustrate what I'm talking about, we will use our fictitious lender, John's Bank, once again.

I have an account with John's Bank. Let's say that it's a car loan for $25,000. I've had the account for a little over a year and I've already paid that balance down to $19,100. I've never missed a payment. All in all, it's a great account because it shows that I can responsibly manage an auto loan. It's definitely helping my credit scores.

But wait. It's not actually helping my credit scores, because the lender has chosen not to report it to any of the three credit reporting agencies. And if it's not on my credit reports, it doesn't help my scores. In fact, nobody knows that I even have an auto loan except the lender and me. The story continues...

I mail my monthly payment in, but it gets lost in the mail. By the time the lender calls me asking why I didn't make my payment the due date has past. I write them another check and send it off. All is well, right? Maybe not. This lender has a policy that they do report late payments to the credit bureaus. So, now the account is showing up on my credit reports, but it's showing that it was late last month. Now it's hurting my scores.

Is that fair? I never got any credit on my credit reports for the first year of on-time payments, but the minute I miss a payment (through no fault of my own), that gets reported for all to see for the next seven years. Of course it's not fair, but that's our credit reporting system, completely voluntary and completely dependent upon how a lender reports.

Lenders can choose whose credit reports they'll use to help process your applications. That is, of course, if they want to use a credit report at all. It's not mandatory that lenders pull your credit report. Once the account has been opened, they can choose to report the account or not. And they can choose which credit bureau to report it to. If an account is paid late, they can choose whether or not they will actually report it as being late. All voluntary.

Some lenders will even give their customers the benefit of the doubt and not report them as late until they're several cycles past due. Again, there is no hard and fast rule on how late you have to be before your credit reports hear about it. There are some lenders who don't report late payments at all unless you get several months behind. All voluntary.

There are even some lenders who only report certain information about your account to the credit bureaus. This is bad for consumers because some of the missing information could help raise credit scores if it was being reported. There is a lawsuit pending over some lenders' incomplete reporting practices.

The delay in credit reporting

When you apply for credit and lenders pull your credit report, they will see the most up-to-date information that the credit bureaus have on file. The score they get will be based upon that same information. The problem is that the information being reported by lenders is typically 30 days old. In many cases, it is a full 60 days old.

That means payments, payoffs, charges, credit line increases, or any other account changes that have occurred in the past month will not be reflected in your credit reports and won't be taken into account by credit scoring models. In some cases this can help you, like if you just charged a large amount on your credit cards. But in some cases this can hurt you, like if you just wrote a check and paid off your credit card balance.

The fact that this can help you isn't what I'm concerned about. Rather, I worry about the fact that it can hurt you and more importantly, that you have no control over this. You can't speed up the process. You can't FedEx your payments to the lender and expect that they'll update your accounts any faster than they already do.

All lenders report their customers' account information to the credit bureaus once a month, normally at the end of the billing cycle. That means if your payment reaches them one day after they've sent in their updates, you'll have to wait another 30 days until they send another one to get your account information updated. Even if you write a check and pay off your credit card in full, by the time the next update is sent to the credit bureaus you would have likely purchased something else on your credit cards. That means your credit reports will never reflect that you have paid your balances in full unless you stop using your credit cards for a full 60 days.

This has even become a strategy for consumers who are trying to increase their scores just before a major purchase: Pay off your credit cards and stop using them for two months. That way, the balance reflected on your credit reports is actually your balance. It's just a shame that it takes such a ridiculous strategy – of not using your cards at all for 60 days – to counteract the delay in credit reporting.

This isn't a new problem. It's been this way for decades. The credit bureaus and lenders never thought to improve the process so that credit reports could be updated in real time. It's not as if this is a radical idea. After all, the lender knows immediately whenever you use your credit cards. In fact, each time you charge something, the lender monitors the transaction to make sure that you're not going over your limit or that the purchase is suspicious and possibly fraudulent. So it's not as if lenders can't update a database in real time. The credit bureaus just haven't made this a priority.

The "so-called" investigation

The Fair Credit Reporting Act gives each of us the right to challenge information in our credit files. If the information cannot be verified in a timely manner, it must be removed or changed in favor of the consumer. This process is called "investigation" and must be completed within 30 days from when the credit bureaus receive the dispute from the consumer.

You'd think, as important as credit reports are to so many people, that the system of investigating would be sophisticated. Once again, you'd be very disappointed. The process starts when consumers notice something on their credit reports that they don't recognize or that they disagree with. They contact the credit reporting agencies –via mail, email or telephone– and challenge the information. The credit reporting agencies spring into action and make a notation on the consumer's credit file that the information is under investigation.

What do you think happens next? Is it assigned to a team of investigators who will spend time researching the information, interviewing people, or even looking at clues, all in an effort to determine the validity of the disputed account? Hardly. In what can only be categorized as "What a joke," the credit bureaus will send a letter back to the same lender who reported the disputed item, asking them to either verify that it is being reported correctly or change it.

Remember: This is the same exact company that reported the information (possibly incorrectly) in the first place. All the credit bureau is doing is essentially asking the lender if what it already reported is correct. That's not an investigation. All that is being verified is what the lender already has in its database, which might very well be incorrect. If the lender confirms that what they already sent is correct, then the information stays on file regardless if it is correct or not. What a joke.

It seems to me that the true meaning of an investigation would be for the credit bureaus to ask the lender to do some sort of research into the validity of the information. Was a payment posted incorrectly, was a credit issued, was a bill sent to the wrong address? Information can be incorrect for a dozen different reasons. If you simply look in your "system" just to see if you have the same data that was sent to the credit bureaus, you're not doing the consumer justice.

In a perfect credit world, every single obligation that I pay would be credited to me somehow. That includes paying on time my apartment rent, utilities, cell phone bill, and any other obligation that is not typically reported to the credit bureaus. I've even spoken to some people who feel that tithing is a financial obligation and they want to be given credit for it.

Anytime I charge something, make a payment, or change something on an account of mine, it should be reflected in real time, immediately. This would benefit lenders by giving them a true and accurate credit score as of the moment the consumer applied. It would benefit consumers by giving them credit for up-to-date payments, pay offs, or any other action that is currently reported on a delay that could help their credit scores.

And, finally, whenever I challenge something on my credit report, the investigation should be more than just the simple verification process that is done today. It's simply not good enough. The investigation should be more of an exploratory into the validity of the consumer data. Don't we deserve at least that much?

Chapter 15

Scores, Scores and More Scores!

T his is one of the chapters that's going to lead to more questions. We all know our credit is scored and that lenders and insurance companies use this information to evaluate us and the applications we submit for their review and approval. That's not a secret. What is a secret is the fact that you're being scored so many other times and by so many other scoring models, and you aren't even aware of it.

I did a presentation several years ago. A gentleman from a large national bank was co-presenting with me. He told the audience –all of whom were consumer credit counselors– that in any given year, each one of their credit card customers was scored an average of 57 times. And the vast majority of those scores were something other than the traditional credit risk score that we are all at least somewhat familiar with.

Let's talk about some of the other scores that are used to evaluate you as a customer or as a prospective customer and then we'll go into some more detail about them.

Credit Risk Scores

We're all familiar with credit risk scores. These scores evaluate the information on your credit reports in an effort to give lenders an indication of what kind of a customer you will be. If your credit is good, you'll be considered a good credit risk. If your credit is not so good, you'll be considered something other than a good credit risk. These scores are calculated when you apply and are periodically updated throughout the time you have the account open with the lender. In many cases, your credit card issuers will get your credit risk scores once a month. Or, at the very least, they'll get them once a quarter.

Revenue Scores

There are models that are designed to predict the likelihood of you generating positive credit card revenue. What is important to a credit card issuer is not only the fact that you are going to pay your bills on time, but also that you will generate revenue for them. If you have no chance of generating revenue for them, it is unlikely that you are going to get their best offer or even an approval, despite the fact that you may be a very low credit risk

If you are not generating revenue for them, it's possible that you are a loss for them because you are actually costing them money to be on their books rather than generating positive revenue by using your account and revolving a balance month after month. And as we all know, lenders don't care about you – they care about your money.

All of the credit reporting agencies sell revenue scores or other models that predict the likelihood of you generating positive credit card revenue. Lenders and credit card issuers can also build their own revenue scores internally and use those in addition to other credit scores that they've purchased from the credit bureaus in order to evaluate your revenue potential. These scores are often used in conjunction with other scores, such as the traditional credit risk score, to determine whether or not you are going to get approved for a credit card that you've applied for and according to what terms.

Bankruptcy Scores

Another type of score used by lenders is the bankruptcy score. Bankruptcy scores are designed specifically to predict the likelihood of an applicant or a current customer filing for bankruptcy – either a Chapter 7 bankruptcy or a Chapter 13 bankruptcy. Some people get confused and think that bankruptcy scores are the same as credit risk scores, but they're not. Credit risk scores are designed to predict the likelihood that you will pay your bills poorly but not necessarily poorly enough that you'd end up needing to file for bankruptcy.

As you can imagine, if you are more likely to file for bankruptcy, lenders are going to be less likely to approve your application than if you are highly unlikely to file bankruptcy. Again, all three of the credit reporting agencies sell bankruptcy scores to lenders and almost all lenders either use them or have access to them. As with the use of revenue scores, lenders commonly will use a bankruptcy score in conjunction with another score, such as a credit risk score. That way they get a good feel of your likelihood to pay late and your likelihood to file for bankruptcy.

Response Scores

Another type of scoring model that is used is a response model. Credit card issuers who mail out pre-approved credit card solicitations generally use response models. You and I may call that stuff "junk mail." These are the letters you receive almost every single day that tell you you've been pre-approved or pre-qualified for a credit card.

Credit card issuers send these out as a way of generating new clients and as a way of building their customer base. Almost all credit card issuers spend hundreds of thousands if not millions of dollars studying whether or not the people they are sending the offers to are actually going to respond to them and open a new account. One of the tools they use is the response score.

A response score predicts the likelihood that consumers will actually respond to mail they receive. As you can imagine, the response rate is extremely low. The industry averages around ½ of 1%. So, anything that credit card issuers can do to improve the response rate is definitely worth their time and money.

Attrition Scores

Another type of score that lenders use is called an attrition model. In the lending world, specifically the credit card world, attrition is the gradual erosion of a customer base. Specifically, it's when credit card customers stop using one of their cards (or close an account) in lieu of using another that they've opened somewhere else. This erosion of customers is generally considered to be a cancer in the credit card industry.

Lenders will spend a great amount of time, effort, and money trying to convince you that you should not go to another company or competitor of theirs. One of the ways they identify who they need to be most worried about is by knowing your attrition score. This score predicts the likelihood of you leaving them for another company.

For example, if you opened a credit card and used it frequently for six months and then stopped, you're more likely to have started using another card. These are the types of activity that an attrition score will pick up on and give the credit card issuer some idea that there's a potential problem. You may get a call from the issuers just to touch base, or they may send you some convenience checks in your next statement. They will do all of this with the goal of retaining you as a customer.

Other Scores

So far, all of the scores we've talked about are generated using information from your credit reports. These are all referred to as "credit bureau scores" because of their dependency on your credit data and the fact that you can buy these from the credit bureaus. The scores we're going to talk about next take into account information that is not on your credit reports.

Behavior Scores

A behavior score is normally used by credit card issuers as a way to measure and grade your performance on how you have managed the account you have with them. Rather than looking at your credit reports and determining how you have behaved with all of your other lenders and credit obligations, a behavior score is specifically trying to measure how you have performed with just one account, the one with that specific lender.

The better your behavior score, the more likely you'll receive credit line increases, convenience checks in the mail, and waived late fees if you ever happen make a late payment. It's less likely that the lender will increase your credit limits if your behavior scores are very low. Additionally, the lender could reduce your credit limit when your card comes up for renewal. And, in the worst case possible, the credit card issuer could certainly choose not to renew the card at all because of your poor behavior scores.

Application Scores

Application scores take into account information from your credit application that is not likely to be in your credit reports. This includes the answers to questions like: Are you employed? Are you unemployed? How long have you lived at your current address? What is your salary? How long have you worked in the same industry? How long have you been with the same employer? Do you have a checking or savings account?

These are the types of questions that have some predictive value to the lender, which is why they'll use an application model. People generally don't think too much about their applications when they're filling them out. But, this is one of the purposes of that information – to get your application score. This information is not on your credit reports and it's much easier for a lender to get it from an application than anywhere else.

Collection Scores

A collection score is used by collection agencies to determine whether or not they will be able to collect your past due debts. The collection agency will score an entire group of consumers who are currently in collections and the collection score will rank them according to the "collectability" of each. This gives the collection agency the ability to assign some of the more difficult cases to their most seasoned collectors and assign some of the so-called "low hanging collection fruit" to some of the newer, less experienced collection agents.

All of the credit reporting agencies sell collection scores to collection agencies. Some collection agencies even build some of their own custom collection scores in-house for their own use. If your collection score is so low that a collection agency feels it will never collect any money from you, the agency may not spend any telephone time trying to recover the debt. Instead, they may simply report the account to the credit reporting agencies – one, two, or all three of them, – and send letters to you in an effort to collect the debt with the least amount of time, effort, and cost involved.

Transaction Scores

A transaction score is probably the most frequent score that is calculated, and consumers have no idea it's being done. A transaction-scoring model scores every single one of the transactions that you make using one of your credit cards.

The goal of a transaction score is to determine whether or not the lender should approve the transaction that you're trying to complete. Say, for example, that you are at a gas station. You slide your card through the credit card reader to buy $50 worth of gasoline. Prior to the lender's approval of the transaction, it will be scored to determine whether or not it is a fraudulent transaction, whether the transaction will cause you to exceed your credit limit, and whether there is some other reason why the lender would want to decline the transaction prior to allowing it to take place.

A very common type of transaction score determines whether or not the transaction is fraudulent. We've all gotten phone calls from our credit card issuers asking us if we were the actual customer at a store where we were said to have purchased something. The reason you're getting the phone call is because a "fraud score," a type of transaction score, has kicked out the transaction and has identified it as being possibly fraudulent.

This could happen if most of your purchases are made in one state or one area and all of a sudden you're making a purchase half way across the country. This could be taken as a sign that your credit card may have been stolen and is being used fraudulently. That will generally kick the transaction over to a fraud agent with the credit card issuer. The agent will call you to verify whether or not you are in fact the person making the purchases.

The vast majority of your scored transactions never lead to anything because the vast majority of credit card transactions are completely legitimate. Whether you use your credit card once a month or 200 times a year, each of these transactions is scored.

Chapter 16
The Top 12 Credit Myths

F irst off, what is a credit myth? I believe that the credit myth is a commonly held belief about credit reporting or credit scoring that has taken on an air of legitimacy however incorrect it may be. I believe that the press causes most credit myths. The press distributes incorrect information through articles that are picked up by national publications and published as factual. What do you think when you read something in the *Wall Street Journal* or the *New York Times* or the *Atlanta Journal Constitution*? You make the assumption that it's accurate and that the reporter has done enough research on the topic, so the information must be 100% correct. You'd be very surprised and shocked to learn that this is simply not the case. In fact, in the 15 years that I've been a part of the consumer credit industry, I can tell you I've never read an article that has been 100% accurate on all things regarding credit reporting and credit scoring.

Another source of credit myths are the so-called 'credit experts.' There are a whole slew of self-proclaimed credit experts who have spent no time working for any of the credit reporting agencies or any of the companies that build credit scoring models, yet they have fashioned themselves as somehow being credit experts. In an effort to sell products and services, these so-called credit experts write books, go on television shows, create infomercials and somehow distribute products and services to consumers that may contain information and advice that isn't 100% accurate because it hasn't come from the industry. They are researching it from the outside.

And in many cases, it isn't even them doing the research – instead, it's coming from a team of researchers. They are just the marketing face or, better put, the celebrity. I believe they are an even bigger problem than the press because these people are motivated by the enormous amount of money they make selling information to consumers. Whether or not the information is completely accurate is another story, and might not be the goal of these salespeople. The problem is that when the consumer tries to act upon the information they've purchased from one of these "experts," they may actually hurt their credit instead of helping it.

However, the biggest source of credit myths is lenders giving inaccurate information to their customers. Lenders, including car dealers and mortgage lenders, tell people information that is flat-out inaccurate when it comes to credit reporting and credit scoring. I can't think of a bigger source of incorrect information than the lenders.

Now, don't get me wrong; I have no problem with someone becoming a credit expert and making a fantastic living selling products and services to consumers. I also don't have any problem with lenders, car dealers, or mortgage lenders. The problem I have is anyone who gives consumers advice on a topic as serious as credit scoring when they are simply not experts. Example: I'm not a doctor, and as such I will never give you medical advice. You should never ask for medical advice from me. Sure, I can make some general assumptions about medical health that people will believe because they make common sense. Am I a medical expert? Not even close. Should anyone listen to any medical advice that I give him or her? Absolutely not.

It's the same in the credit world. People who haven't spent serious time in important positions at the credit reporting agencies and people who haven't spent years building and teaching consumers and lenders about credit scoring models are simply not qualified to talk about the topic. The majority of books, courses, and newsletters about credit and credit reporting and credit scoring are written and sold by people who haven't spent even one single day working for a credit reporting agency, a lender, or a company that builds credit scoring models. Yet they consider themselves qualified to write a book on the topic and expect consumers to follow their advice.

Now that we've identified where these myths come from, we'll go over some of the more commonly held credit myths and debunk them.

Myth 1. Close credit card accounts if you're not using them

This is probably the worst piece of advice that anybody can follow. When we're talking about credit cards, we're referring to anything plastic inside of your wallet – this includes Visa, MasterCard, and any traditional credit cards issued by credit card issuers, as well as any cards issued at retail outlets where you can purchase clothing or other types of goods. This also includes gas cards issued by lenders so that you can buy gasoline at their gas stations. This does not include check or debit cards, as those are not real credit cards.

Closing your credit card accounts might be a great strategy to avoid identity theft. However, when it comes to improving your credit scores, it is probably the worst thing you can do. The myth in this case is that your unused credit limit (also called "open to buy") is considered bad by lenders and therefore hurts your credit scores. Research has shown that consumers who DO have a large amount of unused credit actually pose less of a credit risk than consumers who have a smaller amount of "open to buy."

Closing unused credit cards can absolutely and in most cases WILL lower your credit scores. The reason is that it can negatively impact your revolving utilization, which is one of the most important measurements in your credit score. We've talked about that in other chapters of this book. To have a very low or respectable utilization, you have to have low balances in proportion to your credit limits. By closing unused credit cards, you cause that account to be excluded from the utilization calculation. This can spike your utilization percentage, which can cause your credit scores to drop drastically in a very short amount of time.

If your credit cards have been stolen, by all means call the credit card issuers and have them close that account and reissue a new card. However, if you are in the process of rebuilding or establishing your credit and trying to improve your credit scores, then closing your credit accounts is definitely not a good idea. Anyone who tells you to do this doesn't know the first thing about credit scoring.

Myth 2. Avoid credit after a bankruptcy or some other credit disaster

Let's set the record straight on something. Credit use is not bad. Credit **abuse** is bad. Credit **avoidance** is bad. Anytime you use credit, you are giving credit scoring models something to look at and evaluate. If you establish and use credit responsibly, your credit scores will be good. If you don't establish and use credit responsibly, your credit scores will be bad. If you avoid using credit, you're not giving credit scoreing models anything to evaluate and therefore your scores will not recover as quickly as someone who jumps right back in and establishes new credit and manages it properly.

The myth in this case is that if I avoid credit, my credit scores will somehow be good or will somehow recover faster than if I started using credit again. This is absolutely incorrect. The best thing you can do if you're trying to establish or rebuild your credit after having some sort of credit-damaging event is to jump right back into the game and re-establish credit. Prove to the credit scoring models that you can manage your credit properly this time around. This is the best thing that you can do to quickly rebuild your credit and establish good credit scores.

There are some so-called "credit and finance experts" that try to convince people that living debt-free is a good thing. The problem with that strategy is that every single one of us will eventually need to fall back on our credit reports and credit scores. Whether we need to refinance a home, buy a new home, finance a college education, get a job, or even get insurance, there are some things in life that we simply can't avoid. We will need a good credit history to prove to someone else that we can responsibly manage our credit obligations.

Think of how you were treated when you were 18 years old and tried to establish credit for the first time after not having any credit at all. Lenders treat consumers that have no credit or who have exited the credit environment worse than they treat consumers who have debt but manage it properly. So don't avoid credit. Establish credit. Use what you need and manage it properly. Pay your bills on time. Don't over-utilize your credit cards and don't excessively shop for credit. Heed this advice and you will have solid credit scores.

Myth 3. Paying your bills on time is the best way to get a good score

This is a fact; however, it's a misleading fact that's missing valuable context. Paying your bills on time is important. However, it makes up only a small amount of the points in your credit scores – one-third to be exact. In order to earn and maintain solid credit scores, it is important that you perform well in all of the reported areas in addition to just paying your bills on time.

This means responsible use of credit, and only shopping for credit when it's necessary – not with such irresponsibility as to get 10% off of your purchases at the mall simply because you've opened a new account. Let's put it this way: If you paid your bills on time but did everything else wrong, your credit scores could be just as bad as someone who filed for bankruptcy.

Myth 4. If you correct errors on a report with one credit reporting agency, it will be picked up and corrected by all three

This is absolutely incorrect. The three credit reporting agencies are competitors. They do not share information. They compete like Coke and Pepsi, Republicans and Democrats – they do not share information with each other despite the fact that, in this case, it's for the common good.

If you have information on your credit reports that is incorrect, you'll have to address it independently with each of the three credit reporting agencies. I recognize that this is hugely inefficient, but unfortunately it's the way it is in today's credit environment.

Myth 5. All of your credit reports contain identical information

This myth actually dovetails nicely off of the previous myth. Again, this is incorrect. Since the three credit reporting agencies do not share information and because lenders can voluntarily report to whichever of the three credit reporting agencies that they choose, it's actually very uncommon for a consumer to have the same credit report at all three of the credit reporting agencies. When you apply for a loan other than a mortgage, the lender will pull just one of your three credit reports. This means one of your credit reports now has an inquiry that isn't on the other two. There you have it: inconsistent credit information.

Because of this, your credit scores are going to be different at each credit-reporting agency. In the 16 years that I have been in the consumer credit world, I've never seen three credit reports that are identical, and I've never seen three credit scores that are the same for the same consumer. It simply doesn't happen. This is why, in the mortgage-lending environment, they want to see all three of your credit reports and all three of your credit scores – to make sure that they have a complete picture of your credit risk.

Myth 6. Your salary or your level of education positively or negatively impacts your score

This is simply incorrect. The only information that can go into your credit scores is the information that's on your credit report. And, just because it *can* go into your score doesn't mean that it actually *does* go into them. The information must be predictive and legal, and it must not present any public relations issues.

Your salary is not on your credit report. Your race is not on your credit report. And your level of education is not on your credit report. As such, it cannot be used as a component in the model.

Some people would argue that your salary, race, and level of education have an indirect impact on your credit scores because they play a part in how you establish and manage credit. This is probably true, but the fact remains the same. Race, salary, and level of education are not on your credit reports and therefore do not have any direct impact on your credit scores.

Myth 7. A divorce decree will release you from financial responsibility for an account

It's very important that you understand this one since 50% of us have already gone through a divorce or will do so eventually. The above statement is incorrect and can be one of the most damaging myths if you believe it to be true. Unfortunately, just because the divorce court decrees that either you or your ex-spouse is responsible for an account, the decree does not supersede the original account with the lender.

In many cases, divorce leads to both credit reports and scores being trashed because one or the other party stops paying on the account because he or she feels that they are no longer responsible as ordered by the court. However, the lender does not recognize that the court decree takes you or your spouse off of an account if both of you signed on the line for it as a joint account.

What happens? *Both* credit reports get trashed because the accounts are not paid. They end up being reported as delinquencies on *both* spouses' credit reports. The best way to avoid this is to refinance accounts into one person's name or actually close the account before the divorce takes place. This is definitely not a move that you would typically make, but since you're going through a divorce it's definitely the lesser of two evils.

Myth 8. If you have bad credit, it's a lifelong sentence

It's a good thing this one's a myth. The reality is that your credit reports and credit scores are dynamic. This means that they constantly change. In fact, your credit scores will change every time information on your credit reports change. That means your credit scores will be different multiple times every single month.

As your delinquencies get older, your scores will naturally improve. This is because bad information loses negative value as it ages. And if you have established new credit and managed it responsibly, your credit scores will improve fairly quickly.

Myth 9. Check cards or debit cards will help rebuild your credit

This, again, is incorrect. Check cards and debit cards are really nothing more than plastic checks. They are connected to your checking account and are not true credit card accounts, despite the fact that they may have a Visa or MasterCard logo. Sometimes parents think that simply giving their children a debit or check card will help them establish credit. Sorry, but it doesn't work like that.

Myth 10. Opening new credit cards and transferring balances will help your scores because you're hiding your balances

What a joke. This will most likely lower your credit scores because when you open a new account it will result in a credit inquiry and the new account hitting your credit reports. Just because you transfer a balance from one credit card to another credit card doesn't mean that it will be off of your credit report. And as you have probably learned from reading this book, anything on your credit report is fair game to the credit scoring models. That includes any balance transfers.

Some people also believe, incorrectly, that if you distribute your balances more equally among all of your credit cards that this somehow improves your credit scores as well. This is also incorrect. Most score measurements that look at your credit card debt look at your credit card debt in aggregate. That means if you have $10,000 in credit card debt spread across ten cards or $10,000 in debt on one card, it's still $10,000. So don't play games with the credit scoring models and move balances from here to there thinking such actions will somehow help you. It definitely will *not*, and in many cases it will actually lower your scores.

Myth 11. Paying or settling a negative account such as a judgment, lien, or charge off will remove that item from your credit reports

Once again, this is incorrect. Paying or settling a negative account will only update the balance on that account to show it has been paid. If it's a judgment, it will show that it has been satisfied. If it's a lien, it will show that it has been released. And if it is a collection or charge off, it will show that it has been paid in full and now has a zero balance.

This does not mean that your credit score will go up. In fact, your credit score probably won't change at all. This is confusing to consumers and sometimes irritating because the consumer makes the assumption that their balance on the negative account is what's causing their scores to be lower. The reality is that what's causing the score damage is the fact that you have the negative item in the first place. Not so much the balance on that item. So just because you have a charged off account that's been paid in full ($0), don't think that's any better than having a charged off account with a $10,000 balance. What's most important is the fact that you have a charged off account in the first place.

Some people also make the assumption that settling the account is somehow better for your credit scores than paying the account in full. That's not the case. In fact, settling an account is considered negative just like missing payments is considered negative. Settling an account means that you have made an agreement with the creditor and that they will take less than the full amount and consider the account paid in full. This is called settlement. For example, if you owed someone $1,000 but they agreed to take $500 as payment in full, that's considered a settlement. If a settlement is listed on your credit report, it is considered just as negative as not paying it at all.

Some companies actually market services where they can settle your tax liens for less than the full amount. Although that may be a smart financial move, don't think it helps your credit scores because it simply does not.

Myth 12. You should try to get old, good accounts removed from your credit reports once they have been paid in full or closed

This last myth is one of the most potentially damaging if you believe it to be true. Some people think that when an account is closed or paid in full, they should argue with the credit reporting agencies and try to get them to remove it. Trying to get old, good accounts removed from your credit reports is actually a VERY bad idea. You never want anything positive to be removed from your credit reports because that information always helps your credit scores. In fact, having a lot of old, good accounts will not only help your credit scores but it will also ensure that your credit scores don't fluctuate wildly from month to month.

The more good accounts you have on your credit reports, the more stable your credit score will be. In fact, the best scenario would be for you to have numerous pages of good accounts on your credit reports, no matter how old they are. Then, because all of the overwhelming good credit history that you currently have, it would be very unlikely that applying for new credit or taking on a lot of new debt or maybe even missing payment could have a negative impact on your score. Your good, old credit would buffer and protect you.

Chapter 17
Important Tidbits

I n Chapter 17 we're going to talk about some concepts that just aren't voluminous enough to be their own chapters. These things are very important, however, so we're going to combine them all into one chapter.

How to establish and re-establish credit

There are several situations where establishing or re-establishing credit is a necessity. For example, if you moved to this country from another country, it is very likely that your credit history is not going to transfer over to the U.S. credit reporting agencies. The one exception is if you're moving here from Canada.

Equifax and TransUnion are in both the U.S. and Canada, and they do have the ability to share credit files across the border. However, if you move to the U.S. from any other country, you will have to start your credit history from scratch. Therefore, you will have to establish yourself with U.S. lenders.

If you experienced some sort of tragic life event that damaged your credit, such as a divorce, loss of job, a death in the earning family, or even some sort of major medical catastrophe that wiped out your savings, it will be important that you re-establish credit. The difference between re-establishing credit and establishing credit for the first time is that when you re-establish credit, you have a past credit history that is going to hinder your efforts. When you establish credit for the first time, you're essentially starting from scratch. There's nothing good or bad to show anyone.

There are three things that I suggest people do when trying to re-establish their credit. The first is to use secured credit cards. A secured credit card is a credit card where you make a deposit with the bank and they issue you a credit card. The credit limit is the same amount as your deposit. So, if you give the bank $1,000 and they give you a secured credit card, your credit limit will be $1,000.

This is a great loan product for them because if you don't pay your bill, they'll simply take the money out of the deposit you've already made. It's almost the equivalent of a prepaid credit card because they already have your money. Secured credit cards normally have very high interest rates and fees, so they aren't a very good product for consumers who already have established a solid credit history. But for consumers who have poor credit and are trying to re-establish, they are a necessary evil. With a secured card, you're simply buying the credit with the deposit you are making. When talking to your bank about a secured credit card, be sure that they report your account to all three of the credit reporting agencies. Remember: If it's not on your credit reports, your scores cannot benefit from your responsible management.

When shopping for a secured card, there are a few things that you need to be aware of before you make your decision. First, you want to find a company with the lowest interest rates and fees possible. You're still probably going to pay higher than 20% and you will still have to pay some sort of account establishment or monthly fees, but that's all right. Just shop around and try to find the one with the lowest fees.

The next item: Since you're in a score improvement mode, you want to make sure you make your payments on time. You do not want new late payments to litter your credit reports or it's going to be more difficult for your credit scores to improve. Take advantage of technology and sign up for automatic electronic bill pay. And don't ever make the assumption that just because they have your money on deposit that it's ok to miss a payment or pay late. It isn't! You're in score improvement mode, and that means you have to do it better and cleaner than anyone else. All eyes are upon you.

Ok, now that you've opened the account, you'll want to keep your balance at no more than 10% of the credit limit. That means if you have a $1,000 credit limit, you don't ever want your balance to go over $100. Keeping your balance below 10% of the credit limit is great for your credit scores. Anything higher than 10% is going to cause your scores to be lower than they could be.

After making on-time payments for 24 - 36 months, some secured card issuers will convert the card into a traditional unsecured credit card and return your deposit. Some issuers will require that you make timely payments for more than three years and some will even require that you request that the secured card be converted to an unsecured card. Eventually, when you don't need the secured card any longer, don't close the account. Remember: Having an unused credit limit is always good for your credit scores. So, just pay off the balance and don't use the card, but don't close it.

Another type of account that can be used to re-establish credit is a retail store card. These are the cards that are offered by retail stores such as Target or Macy's. These cards are generally very easy to get because their credit qualifications are very liberal. It doesn't mean that anybody can get them, but it does mean that people who have poor credit generally have an easier time getting a retail store card than they do getting a high-limit Visa or MasterCard.

Retail store cards are good because the credit limits are generally very low, making it difficult to run up a lot of debt. This can be a double-edged sword, however, because even charging only a few hundred dollars can cause your utilization to be very high, which can lower your credit scores. So, when you do open a retail store credit card, be sure to keep your balances to 10% or less of the credit limit, just like you do with your secured cards. I know that this makes the card difficult to use, but you're not in a position where you can take on a lot of new debt. You're rebuilding.

Another option for re-establishing credit is opening an account with a credit union. Credit unions are great because they generally treat their customers much better than banks. Credit unions refer to their customers as "members" and the treatment is much more in line with how you'd expect a "member" to be treated. At a bank, you're nothing more than a number.

Most lending decisions made by a credit union are made locally, perhaps even by someone at the branch. At a bank, someone in the risk management department predetermines the lending decision. This is called "centralized lending" because the branches have no authority to make the decision. It works just fine for banks, but customers get lost in the shuffle.

At a credit union, you may even be able to talk to the decision maker when you submit an application and explain any situation that you may have regarding your credit. You may be able to convince the credit union to treat you differently than if you were applying online. The only drawback with credit unions is that they typically don't report to all three of the credit reporting agencies. Most of the time, they report to at least one, however, so a credit union account will help your credit scores somewhat.

The right and wrong credit

Believe it or not, there's a right type and a wrong type of credit. You can actually open an account with a company, pay it on time, manage it responsibly and still have that account lower you scores simply because of the identity of the lender. In this case, I'm talking specifically about finance companies.

A finance company is generally considered the "last resort" in the lending world. Their interest rates are very high and they typically target high-risk consumers who can't get a loan with a bank or a credit union. A finance company is happy to do business with high-risk consumers because they make more money if they can charge someone 29% than a bank charging somebody 5.5% on the same loan.

Remember, lenders aren't in the business of making friends. They're in the business of making money. They don't care about your situation; they don't care about your excuses. All they care about is that you make your payments.

Most people with good credit avoid finance companies because their rates are so high. However, consumers who have poor credit or who are trying to re-establish credit may have to use finance companies for a certain period of time. They'll do this until they can get back on their feet and earn the right to do business with more reputable lenders who will give them more competitive interest rates.

An exception is when people accidentally sign up for accounts with finance companies. I bet you're thinking, "How in the world could I accidentally open an account with a finance company?" You might want to sit down for this one. It's going to really tick you off.

This is actually very common. Think about when you go to a big box retailer or furniture store and you take advantage of one of their "12 months same as cash" or "No payments for 36 months" offers. Most of these retailers don't have their own bank and are not lenders. However, almost all of them have partnerships with finance companies, so when you sign up for credit, you're actually opening an account with their finance company partner.

The finance company pays the furniture company for the merchandise, and you pay the finance company (eventually) for the amount that you borrowed. The bad news is that the account you opened with the finance company will probably show up on your credit reports and may lower your credit scores. It's such a shame because people who have great credit take advantage of those "same as cash" offers and wind up with scores that aren't as high as they could be. They're usually perplexed as to why. Now they know.

Of course, this isn't something the folks at the retail stores know about or would even be able to explain to the average consumer. The right types of lenders to do business with are banks, credit unions, reputable auto lenders, and credit card issuers. Avoid finance companies.

Do I even qualify for a score?

Something that you may find interesting is that not every consumer is assigned a credit score. That means their credit files don't have a sufficient amount of information to qualify them to be scored by the credit-scoring models. This is definitely not good news. When you go to apply for a loan and the lender is unable to get your credit score, they will have to treat your application much differently than they normally would.

This can lead to a much longer application review process. In some cases, they could decline you simply because they don't want to take the time to process the application manually.

In order to be "scoreable," your credit reports must meet three qualifications:

- •• Your credit files can't have any sort of "deceased" indicator on it. You may laugh about this, but it's more common than you think. If you have a joint account with someone that has passed away, it is very probable that the lender will report the account as belonging to a deceased person. And since you're a joint holder of the account, that notation can show up on your credit files too. If it does, you won't be able to be scored.

➤➤ You have to have at least one account that has been open for at least three to six months. This is determined based upon the opening date of the account. Remember, you only need one of these accounts.

*This criteria is specific to the FICO credit score.

➤➤ And lastly, you have to have at least one account that has been updated in the last three to six months. This is determined based upon the date reported of an account.

*This criteria is specific to the FICO credit score.

One account can qualify your file under the final two requirements. If you have an account that has been open for ten years and was updated last month, and you don't have a deceased indicator on your credit files, you will get a score. If you are new to the country or you are re-establishing credit or are establishing credit for the first time, it's going to take some time for your credit file to be scoreable. When you open your first account, your credit file will not qualify for a score for three to six months.

You don't need to buy your credit scores. Here's a secret way to find out what they are (kind of).

Currently, there is no way to get all of your legitimate credit scores for free. But, there is a way to get an idea of what your scores are without having to buy them. I call this a "score proxy," and it involves the pre-approved offers that you get in the mail.

The offers you get in the mail from credit card issuers are a great way to get an idea of what your credit score is. Remember, there is a lot of thought that goes into these offers, and they don't just send the really good credit offers to everyone. Your score has to be good enough to qualify you for these offers.

If you're getting offers in the mail of the Titanium and Platinum variety with very high credit limits, you can be confident that your scores are pretty good. However, if you're getting credit card offers from nonprime lenders, lenders that you've never heard of, or lenders that are offering you credit cards with very low credit limits, it's very likely that your credit scores are not as good as you think they are and may need some improvement.

First things first

What is the first thing you should do after you finish reading this book? First and foremost: no knee-jerk reactions please. It is very likely that if you have something wrong with your credit files, they can be corrected fairly easily by just working with the credit reporting agencies. It's very important that you don't go out and start taking actions you think should improve your credit without knowing why your credit isn't perfect in the first place. It's very natural to want to try to improve your credit. Along with poor credit management decisions, knee-jerk reactions can also result in lower credit scores and irreparable damage. So, everyone repeat after me: No knee-jerk reactions!

The first thing that I suggest you need is what I call a "credit report diagnostic." You can do this by obtaining all three of your credit reports and determining where you stand as of right now. You can do this for free thanks to the new Federal law that requires all of the three credit reporting agencies to provide you with one free copy of your credit report each year. You won't get a score with these credit reports, but that's not really necessary.

Once you get your credit reports, the first thing you should look for is anything that you don't recognize. Identity theft is a huge problem in this country, and one of the first things that can happen if you've been a victim is that your credit reports become polluted with fraudulent inquiries and accounts. As you are reviewing your credit reports, look for accounts and inquiries that you don't recognize or don't remember opening.

Once you've determined that all of the information on your credit reports is accurate, your next step is to determine what your credit scores are and what you can do to improve them if they're low or what you can do to maintain them if they're already good.

The only problem is that none of the legitimate credit scores are available for free, so this may take an investment on your part. However, if you're in the market for a big-ticket item like a house or a car, or if you're really curious to know what your credit scores are and how to improve them, the investment is probably worth it.

There are a few places online where you can get your legitimate FICO® credit scores, the credit score that was developed by the Fair Isaac Corporation. Fair Isaac's consumer website, which is www.myfico.com, is a great source. You can also find FICO scores at Equifax's consumer website which is www.equifax.com and at one of TransUnion's consumer websites which is www.transunioncs.com.

When you are ordering your credit scores, you will also get something called Score Factors. These are the top reasons why your scores aren't higher. Generally, these will be very specific to the items on your credit report that cost you the most points. For example, if you have filed bankruptcy, the number one item on your credit report that's keeping you from having higher scores is probably that public record – bankruptcy.

If you have a lot of credit card debt and you're highly utilized, the number one factor will probably be that fact that your proportion of balances to credit limits is too high and is causing your scores to not be as high as they could be. Pay close attention to the score factors because they truly are a road map to a strategy that you can implement to earn higher scores. Higher scores mean lower interest rates, lower insurance premiums, and better overall treatment from lenders. This all relates back to your credit files.

If you notice anything on your credit reports you feel is inaccurate, the good news is that as a U.S. consumer you have the right to challenge anything on your credit reports. This is a protection afforded to you under the Fair Credit Reporting Act. You have the right to challenge any item. The credit reporting agencies have to validate it within 30 days of receiving your dispute or they have to change it or remove it. Just be sure to only challenge information that you know is incorrect. You should never challenge information that you know is accurate.

Chapter 18

What are You Trying to Accomplish?

Think of all the reasons that could be driving the way you manage your credit. It's certainly possible that your reasons might be different then mine. If that is true, why is it that so many people offer advice about the best way to manage credit? The truth is, we should manage our credit the way that best meets our needs. There is no "one-size fits all" solution.

Think about someone who is trying to improve a poor credit score. Now think of someone who is trying to avoid identity theft. Now think of someone who is trying to maintain an already good credit score. These people are going to use three completely different strategies because their goals are completely different. And, their credit scores are going to react very differently to each strategy. Let's talk about some goals people have with respect to their credit management.

Managing your credit with the goal of improving a poor credit score

In order to improve a poor credit score, Step #1 is to identify exactly why the score isn't higher in the first place. This may seem very simplistic, but it's very important. My low credit scores could be caused by very different factors than your low credit scores. It's not always because we have both missed payments. There is never a blanket response to the question: "How do I improve my credit scores?"

Strategies for improving a credit score will be different, and in many cases, very different. My case could require that I do nothing more than pay down some of my revolving debt, while your case might require that you open new accounts. Someone else's case may require that the person sit on the sidelines until the delinquencies age a few months.

In my example, all I'd really have to do is write some checks and pay down some of my balances. My scores will go up by doing so. However, for you, since you have to establish a few new accounts, you're going to have to go out and shop for credit, which is going to cause a few credit inquiries and some new accounts to hit your credit reports. Normally that would lower your credit scores, but in your unique case the net affect of your actions could actually raise your scores.

The immediate reaction to both of our actions is going to be very different. You can't simply give blanket advice to large groups of people and expect it to work for every single one of them. Their situations could all be very different, and any advice you give to them could help some and hurt the rest.

Managing your credit with the goal of maintaining a good credit score

You have to be very careful when you're trying to maintain already good credit scores. In most cases, you don't have to take a lot of action, but the wrong actions could be costly. Obviously it's going to be much easier to maintain a good score than it is to improve a poor score. And, similar to the strategy for improving a poor score, the key to maintaining good scores is to understand why your scores are so good in the first place.

Credit scores are going to act like water and are going to take the path of least resistance. Credit scores that are very good are much more susceptible to downward score movement than lower scores. If you already have a good score, that's fantastic. However, don't celebrate too much just yet because with one false step, your credit scores could fall 100 points or more.

Most of the time people who have very good scores have them because of a couple of things. First, they make all their payments on time and they've managed to avoid negative information like public records and collections. Second, they've managed their existing credit very well, meaning they aren't in an excessive amount of debt. And when it comes to shopping for credit, they only do so when it's absolutely necessary. They don't excessively shop for credit and they don't open accounts at the mall in exchange for 10% off their purchase.

One of the dangerous things that someone with great credit scores can do is become unsatisfied with them. One of the realities of credit scoring is that you don't have to have a perfect score (850) in order to get the best offers from lenders and insurance companies. Yet there are people who are dissatisfied with anything but a perfect score, so they continue to try unproven and dangerous strategies thinking that they will improve their scores even more. Take a word from the credit wise: If your scores are all around 750, leave them alone. Every lender in the country already thinks you're perfect. Despite the fact that your scores are 100 points from being perfect, you don't need to do anything. You won't get a better offer at 850 than you got at 800, or even 750 for that matter.

Managing your credit with the goal of avoiding identity theft

I'm sure everyone reading this has either heard of someone being a victim of identity theft or perhaps has even been a victim himself or herself. One of the ways to avoid identity theft is to limit the amount of new credit that you obtain and pare down the number of credit cards you currently have. Unfortunately, people tend to overreact if they think they have been victims of identity theft. In many cases, this overreaction is to the detriment of their credit scores.

Obviously an identity thief can't use a closed credit card, so closing an account you don't use anymore is the best defense against credit card abuse. But, closing credit cards will also wreak havoc on your credit scores. So if you're in the process of trying to buy a home or trying to buy a car, that strategy will actually *hurt* your ability to get approved at the best interest rates. However, it is a great strategy if you're trying to avoid becoming a victim of credit card fraud.

This is perhaps the best example of how two different strategies will have drastically different effects on your credit scores. Think long and hard about the identity theft strategy before executing it. It could hurt you.

Managing your credit with the goal of getting out of debt

Some people believe that you should live as debt-free as possible. This is fine; however, you have to understand that having almost no debt isn't necessarily a good thing for your credit scores. Credit-scoring models like to see that you've managed debt responsibly, not that you've avoided debt.

If you have no debt and have no history of managing debt, your credit scores are going to suffer. They will not be as strong as the scores of someone who has debt, even a lot of debt, and manages it responsibly. It's unfortunate that so many people try to manage debt by paying off all of their accounts and then closing them so they can't be used any longer. Consumers who do this will suffer if they ever want to start using credit again. Because of their lack of recent credit experience, they might see their credit applications denied or they may be offered unattractive interest rates.

Chapter 19

Scorecards

T his chapter could best be defined as advanced credit scoring information. It's a peek behind the curtain of the scoring world, and it will give you an idea of how the process of scoring a credit file begins.

When most people hop into their cars, they turn the key in the ignition and drive off. They don't really think too much about what's happening under the hood. There are hundreds of moving parts that have to work in unison for a car to perform properly. The same is true with credit scoring models. When a credit report is pulled from one of the credit reporting agencies, it has to go through the scoring process before it is delivered to the lender. In this chapter, we will take an in-depth look under the hood – this is called Scorecard Assignment.

This is one aspect of credit scoring that people generally think is too confusing to even address. My opinion is anything that is this important should be shared with people who are interested in learning more. I'll leave it up to them to determine whether or not it's too confusing.

When a credit report is pulled, the first thing that happens is the credit-scoring model determines which scorecard it will use to actually score the credit report. When you think of a scorecard, don't make it more confusing than it needs to be. A scorecard is nothing more than a set of questions and answers that are asked of your credit report. Based upon the answers to the questions, the scorecard assigns points. Those points are added up and that yields your credit score.

Think of a scorecard used in bowling – it's essentially the same. A bowler scores points by knocking down pins in different frames. At the end of the game, the pins are added up and that's the final score. It's really no different in adding up the points that determine your credit scores. Different components of your credit report are scored separately and then they are all added up. That's your final credit score.

In any decent credit-scoring model, there are at least 10 different scorecards. Each is specifically designed to evaluate the credit risk of a different type of consumer. For example, a consumer who has filed for bankruptcy cannot be scored using the same scorecard as someone who has not filed bankruptcy. A consumer who has had credit for only a few years cannot be scored using the same scorecard as someone who has had credit for more than 20 years.

So, each scorecard is like a set of rules to be applied to different consumers. Think about it this way: someone who is 16 years old cannot drink. That's a rule. On the other hand, someone who is 25 years old is allowed to have alcohol. Those two consumers have a completely different set of rules applied to them simply because of their age. It's the same principle in credit scoring. The facts contained in your credit report will determine the set of rules that are applied to you by the credit scoring models.

Back to the questions that scorecards ask of your credit report. Let's say that one of these questions is: "How many late payments do you have?" The credit report can answer that question in a number of ways. Those choices are called variables because the answer can vary. For example, your credit report may answer that question with "I've had ten late payments" whereas my credit report could answer that question with "I've had one late payment."

Score Characteristic	Variable	Points Earned
How many late payments do you have?	0-2	50 points
	3-9	25 points
	10 or more	20 points

It's very likely that you and I are going to earn a different number of points because our answers are different. And while that question could be asked in all ten of the scorecards, the answers will almost certainly yield a different number of points depending upon which scorecard was used.

The next topic we'll talk about is very complex. It's called "scorecard hop." Scorecard hopping happens when something changes on your credit file and causes you to be scored in a different scorecard than the last time your credit score was calculated. For example, if I have a bankruptcy on my credit file, I'm going to be scored using a bankruptcy-specific scorecard. When that bankruptcy falls off of my credit file, my credit report will be scored using a completely different scorecard designed to evaluate the credit of a bankruptcy-free consumer.

What this means to the consumer is that all the rules change. Just because I scored a 600 today doesn't mean that I'll score 600 tomorrow. Something may have changed on my credit files that caused me to jump from one scorecard to another. This means that all of the scoring rules will change. The questions that are asked of my credit file will change. Even if they are similar or the same as another scorecard, the point values of my answers will be different.

This is one of the reasons why consumers' scores can change so drastically without them expecting it. Consumers may open new accounts or close old accounts thinking that their actions will have very little impact on their credit scores. But in doing so, they may have changed their credit report significantly enough to qualify them for a completely different scorecard. They've "hopped" scorecards.

When scores change dramatically as a result, consumers are often confused. They might attribute the change directly to the opening or closing of the account. This is incorrect. The reality is that the information on their credit file changed enough that it caused them to hop scorecards. Now everything on their files is scored somewhat differently. This can be very problematic to consumers who have a limited amount of information on their credit files. That's because when a credit file is very young or has a limited amount of information on it, any changes are much more drastic as a proportion of the credit file as a whole.

Think about it this way: If you have a credit file with only one account on it and you open up a new account, you will double the number of accounts on your credit file. That's a major change. That kind of change will undoubtedly cause your file to be scored in a different scorecard the second time around.

The older and longer your credit files get, the less likely you'll see drastic changes in your scores due to scorecard hop. After you've had credit for many years, pretty much the only thing you can do to cause drastic changes in your scores is if you have severe delinquencies show up or you take on new credit card debt, or either of these things drop off of your files. For example, say you filed for bankruptcy many years ago. Your file will immediately be scored in a different scorecard when the listing of your bankruptcy comes off your file.

Complex stuff, yes. But you deserve to know.

~~ Conclusion ~~

C redit is boring to talk about – even I recognize that. The purpose of this book isn't to make you an expert on credit and credit scoring. And it certainly isn't an effort to entertain you. The cold hard truth of the matter is that unless you make an effort to accept the fact that credit has a far-reaching impact on you and your financial life, you simply won't get the best everyone has to offer. And, unfortunately, a lot of people choose to go through life not caring enough about their credit.

They'll work hard to make more money and spend countless hours with financial planners strategizing where to put their money, but they won't spend any time grasping the low-hanging financial fruit that is easily obtained by simply functioning efficiently within the credit system. Until now, most people weren't privy to the "rules." Well, you can't use that excuse any longer because you've just been given the key to the credit kingdom by reading this book.

If you spent the same amount of effort changing your credit management practices for the better as you spend watching television, you'd be a richer person. You would be richer not only financially, but also as a resource for family and friends to turn to when it's their time to ask for credit-related advice.

Analogy: Would you drive ten miles out of your way to save a nickel on a gallon of gas? Maybe; maybe not. I wouldn't, because my time is more valuable than the $1.00 I would save. And, I burn that gas off driving the extra 20 miles anyway. But you'd be shocked to learn how many people don't think past the initial value of "a nickel cheaper per gallon." The value isn't the money you'll save on gas; it's the understanding that you shouldn't have made the effort to save it in the first place.

How does this apply to your credit? You can work a second job, buy real estate, play the lottery, or do whatever it is that you do to augment your bottom line, regardless of the risk involved. But there's no guarantee any of that will really work. What I can guarantee you is that if you did a better job managing your credit for the sole purpose of making yourself look better to credit scoring models, you wouldn't need that second job because your loans, credit cards, and insurance policies would be cheaper.

It's not about avoiding credit, closing credit cards, or living without debt. Those are the poor strategies of people trying to make a living by pounding desks, yelling at you through a television set, or selling you book after book about real estate investing. We have the

"The value isn't finding a gas station where you'll save a nickel on a gallon of gas. The value is understanding that you shouldn't have made the effort to save it in the first place."

most sophisticated credit system on the globe, and whether you like it or not, it isn't going to change that much over the next 50 years. I've said this throughout the book: Lenders don't care about you; they care about your money. Lenders aren't interested in making friends; they're interested in you making your payments.

What I've taught you in this book isn't commonly known information. This is information that I've learned from living and working in the credit reporting and credit-scoring world since 1991. Use it, take it to heart, and change your credit management practices so that you can be the one making the bold statement about who will and who will not get your credit and insurance business. Bring them to their knees. Your wallet will thank you for it.